Broken & Restored
THE TRUE STORY OF AN EX-CON WHO LOST HIS
FREEDOM BUT REGAINED HIS FAITH

MICHAEL GAY PARKER

Independently Published

Akron, Ohio

Copyright © 2023 by **MICHAEL GAY PARKER**

All rights reserved. No part of this publication may be reproduced, distributed, or transmitted in any form or by any means, without prior written permission.

Unless otherwise noted: All scripture is taken from the New King James Version®. Copyright © 1982 by Thomas Nelson. Used by permission. All rights reserved.

Michael Gay Parker
P.O. BOX 67341
CUYAHOGA FALLS, OHIO 44222

www.michaelgayparker.com
Email: michaelgayparker@michaelgayparker.com

Broken & Restored/ Michael Gay Parker. -- 1st ed.
ISBN 979-8-218-19753-7

Marcia,

Keep letting your life shine for Jesus!

Marlin G. Parker

5-12-24

DEDICATION

"Trust in the Lord with all your heart and lean not on your own understanding; In all your ways acknowledge Him, And He shall direct your paths."
Proverbs 3:5,6

This book is dedicated to my three daughters and to my dad, Ralph Gay II.

Girls, thank you for showing Daddy what unconditional love looks like. God has marked you for greatness, and I cannot wait to see how He uses your gifts to shake up the world. Always keep Him first.
~Love, Daddy.

Dad, it has been quite a journey without you, but I promise to tell you all about it when we see each other again on that Great Day!
~ Forever in my heart!

FORWARD

Michael Parker and I met several years ago in prison. I noticed him studying his Bible in the dayroom of our block almost every morning. When we began to talk a friendship ensued.

Prison is a difficult place for almost everyone and it was (and still is) a blessing to meet someone like Mike. He is a hard worker, with a keen sense of humor, and has several talents, one of which is writing.

You can believe what is between the covers of this book. If Mike is anything, he is authentic, and his love for the Lord is real. I know deep down he wrote this book to help people. May his story be strength and hope for you, the reader. I know it has been for me.

Regards,

Michael Swiergosz

Table of Contents

CHAPTER 1   INTRODUCTION 13
CHAPTER 2   IN THE BEGINNING 19
CHAPTER 3   PRAYER, DON'T LEAVE HOME WITHOUT IT ... 23
CHAPTER 4   BROKEN 29
CHAPTER 5   FLESH DRIVEN DECISIONS 33
CHAPTER 6   BETRAYED 39
CHAPTER 7   SUFFERING IN SILENCE 43
CHAPTER 8   LOVE, GOD'S UNIVERSAL LANGUAGE 47
CHAPTER 9   THE COST OF SUFFERING IN SILENCE 55
CHAPTER 10 MY WILL BE DONE 59
CHAPTER 11 ROTTEN APPLES 65
CHAPTER 12 GOD, I'M BUSY, LEAVE A MESSAGE 69
CHAPTER 13 I DIDN'T MEAN TO KILL HIM 75
CHAPTER 14 FREE CHOICE 79
CHAPTER 15 TRIGGERED 83
CHAPTER 16 IS THIS HOW I AM GOING TO DIE 91
CHAPTER 17 SIN IS CROUCHING AT YOUR DOOR 107
CHAPTER 18 SATAN'S SINFUL PUPPET 125
CHAPTER 19 STRAY CATS 133
CHAPTER 20 GOD HAS A PLAN 145
CHAPTER 21 INSIDE THE WALLS 155
CHAPTER 22 GOD WILL PROVIDE 159
CHAPTER 23 YOU MATTER TO GOD 163
CHAPTER 24 FORGIVEN 169
CHAPTER 25 WHERE THERE ARE PEOPLE, THERE IS PURPOSE 173
CHAPTER 26 SUBMISSION 177
CHAPTER 27 BLESSED AND HIGHLY FAVORED 183

CHAPTER 28 MATTERS OF THE HEART 187
CHAPTER 29 ANXIETY 191
CHAPTER 30 PROMPTINGS FROM THE HOLY SPIRIT 195
CHAPTER 31 BE THE LIGHT 199
CHAPTER 32 IDENTITY CRISIS 203
CHAPTER 33 DIVINE INTERVENTION 207
CHAPTER 34 JESUS IS THE ANSWER 211
CHAPTER 35 RESTORED 217
ACKNOWLEDGMENTS. 225

CHAPTER ONE

Introduction

I remember the day well. December 6, 2018, will be forever branded on my mind. At 3 a.m. the call came: "Parker, pack it up, you're ridin' out!"

At the sound of my name, I sat up as though someone had thrown cold water on my face. I had mixed emotions: I was not happy about heading to prison, but I was happy to leave that dungeon of a cell. The word *comfortable* was no longer in my vocabulary.

The steel sink and toilet were a single unit. When one was in use it would affect the other. I could not get the thought of possibly drinking toilet water out of my mind, and for that reason drinking from the sink was never an option.

Above the sink was a shiny piece of metal fashioned like a mirror. Only God knows how many times I wished it was glass so I could put myself out of misery.

The mattress, which had been worn down from years of use, was about two inches thick and lay on a steel frame.

Between the toilet and bed was a writing table with its Formica top peeled. I guess whoever defaced it got bored and decided to leave the sides. It was impossible to write on it without something smooth underneath my paper.

The only thing I would miss was a radio that sat flush inside a wall in the cell. Music had always been a key part of my life, and listening to it allowed me to escape, mentally.

A deputy gave me a large paper bag to fill with my belongings so a family member could pick them up. Whatever did not fit, I gave to a few men I had bonded with during my eight months stay at the *Summit County Inn*.

The camaraderie between offenders often left me perplexed. Each time someone was about to leave, most if not all the men would offer words of encouragement. "Keep your head up. You got this, homie," and my exit would be no different. I guess it made sense; we all faced the same struggle.

Many of the men had acquired frequent flyer miles in the legal system and knew what was coming. I, on the other hand, had never been to prison and had no clue what to expect. The only thing I knew about prison was what Hollywood taught me.

After saying my goodbyes, I joined a flock of men in a hallway. The only item allowed on our journey was a Bible. Much to my surprise, I was not the only person with one underarm. Just about every offender toted a *Sword*, not as a weapon to fight the devil, but to store personal phone numbers and addresses.

Our first stop was a holding cell. We piled into the room like clowns in a circus car. The stench of urine on the floor, bad hygiene in the air, and the three-day-old jumpsuit I had on was a quick reminder of just how far I had fallen.

While we waited, a few men spoke of their crimes. Some were guilty of theft, murder, and other heinous crimes I dare not mention, but no matter the severity of their deeds, we were all headed to the same place.

I noticed several men, me included, were quick to judge them, if not verbally then internally. I could tell by the look on some of their faces. I know I began to look at them with disgust.

This is how Satan tricks us. He gets us to compare our sins to someone else's. We need to let God and His Word be judge and jury. It does not matter if you stole a coin and I stole a car, sin is sin in God's eyes. Romans 3:23 (NIV) says, *For all have sinned and fall short of the glory of God.*

Waiting with us was a man named Tim. He was tall, thin, and appeared to be in his early fifties. After completing a thirty-year sentence, and being home for two years, he was arrested at his kitchen table for a crime he said he did not commit. This time he was sentenced to death, but he did not seem too concerned. He was confident the Supreme Court would overturn his conviction on appeal, and his calm demeanor was quite convincing. I knew the battle ahead of Tim would be of epic proportions, so I said a silent prayer on his behalf.

Three hours later we were called from the room. Several deputies, shackles in hand, bound us together at the waist in groups of three.

Next, they shackled our ankles individually.

Finally, we were escorted to a van where we would take an hour-long drive to Lorain Correctional Institution (LORCI). This is where offenders go until they leave for their permanent institution. Due to Tim's sentence, U.S. Marshals took him in a vehicle alone.

Physically, the ride was rough. With each bump, the shackles around my ankles dug into my flesh. I should have had the deputy put the cuffs on top of my socks. Rookie mistake. Spiritually, I was at peace. By this time, I had developed a strong relationship with God. Even though I did not know what I was walking into, I knew He was walking in there with me.

Our escorting deputies, who were twin brothers, appeared to be believers. Before we drove away, both men bowed their head and prayed together. Throughout our commute, the radio played songs telling of God's love. I felt my eyes fill with tears on several occasions.

Sitting behind me was a man in his sixties who was about to serve two years for a gambling related offense. He knew most of the songs and sang the entire time. The atmosphere in the van shifted to a holy one thanks to the deputies letting their light shine for Jesus.

The closer we got to the prison, the more nervous I became. By the time we pulled onto the property, my stomach had formed a giant knot.

The deputies turned in their guns as another officer came out and searched the van. He looked under the hood and then walked around with a long-handled mirror, checking the van's undercarriage.

Once cleared, the deputies returned, and we proceeded through the gate. I shook my head and whispered "My Lord" as I marveled at the vast amount of razor wire. If someone managed to get over the first fence, the electric fence behind it would literally blow their mind. It was in this moment that I realized I was not leaving until I was told.

How did I get to this point? What warning signs did I ignore? How did I attend church for over twenty-five years and end up in prison?

It is with complete humility that I share my story. It is a story full of failures, fears, tragedies, triumphs, and the power of God's grace and mercy.

I entered prison broken, but I left restored.
~ Amen.

CHAPTER TWO

IN THE BEGINNING

The summer of 1983 was a hot one in Cleveland, Ohio. Government housing lacked the luxury of central air, and just a thought of sitting indoors would almost melt one's brain. The dry, stagnant heat made one feel as if they were being cooked inside a crockpot set on high. To make matters worse, Mom was pregnant. She had already given birth to my half-sister from an earlier relationship, and I would be her first son.

At the news of their pregnancy, Mom and Dad rushed to a courthouse and married. They wanted to develop a solid home structure before I arrived and did just that.

On August 13th, when I entered the world, I was surrounded by love. My dad, Ralph Gay II, was the first among his siblings to have a child. This made me a hit within the family. Not only did I inherit Dad's and Granny's bushy eyebrows, but their dimples as well. The deep depressions, which sat in my chubby, chipmunk cheeks, made me a perfect candidate to be pinched, poked, and prodded.

However, my time in the spotlight was short-lived. Exactly one year and nine days later my brother was born. Not only were we close on a calendar but in appearance as well. I cannot count the times people would ask if we were twins. It did not help that Mom loved to dress us alike.

Like most brothers, we had our moments. One time while visiting Granny, she noticed the room we were in was extremely quiet for two energetic boys. When she came to investigate, she found us watching TV... as I sat on my brother's head. Don't ask me how, but I had him pinned down and was using his head as a chair. Granny and I still laugh about that today.

If you wanted to know what Dad looked like, all you had to do was look at his boys. We were spitting images of him.

Buried below Dad's exterior was his heart of gold. He found pleasure in rooting for the underdog and making others laugh. Playing the congas and bongos was just one of his hobbies. He was not bad on the eyes either. He kept in great shape and resembled Apollo Creed from the movie *ROCKY* (before he got beat up). He loved our family immensely and was willing to go to any length necessary to protect us. Sadly, none of those things kept my parents together. They divorced two and a half years after I was born.

After the divorce, Mom began dropping us off at Granny's so she could work. When Granny was unavailable, members of Mom's family would watch us. This was an extreme culture shock because the dynamics of both families were drastically different.

If I had to compare each side to a TV show, Dad's would be *Family Matters*. They had great communication skills and were always kind to one another. Even to this day, I have yet to see them argue. I am not saying it did not happen; I am saying it never happened around me.

Mom's family was more like *The Real Housewives of Atlanta*. I dreaded being around them because of the constant drinking, arguing, and fist fighting. Being around them as a child made me anxious. I missed Granny even more during those times. Even as a child, I knew she possessed a peace beyond my understanding (Philippians 4:7 KJV).

Granny was a God-fearing woman. She believed His Word and followed it as best she could, not just on Sundays but every day. One might take her 5-foot stature for weakness, but my granny was tough! Raised in Marengo, Alabama, when racism was all around, she had no choice but to be tough if she were to survive. Planting crops, picking cotton, raising and killing livestock gave her the skills she would need to raise six children.

When it came to us grandkids, she taught us to respect God. Before each meal, we knew to turn off the TV, wash our hands, and then gather at the table. We knew better than to let a crumb of food enter our mouths until Granny thanked God for providing. It was family time, and the dining room table was where she would plant seeds of God's love in us. She also believed in godly discipline and would distribute it when needed, but oftentimes just a look would suffice.

The school I attended was up the street from Granny's home. The trek entailed crossing a busy highway and could be dangerous for an adult and fatal for a child. Thankfully, I always had a chaperone.

One time I got out of class and was surprised to see Dad had come to pick me up. I loved these kinds of surprises. He was my superhero, and I loved showing him off to my friends. As we walked home, I found myself skipping with excitement as the contents in my book bag danced around. If danger dared to show its face, I knew Dad would discreetly use his superpowers to protect us. When I looked at him, I always had a sense of security, but this day something was off.

While waiting to cross the busy road, Dad looked at me, extended his arm, and said, "Here, taste this." I had seen him with this item countless times and was overjoyed when he wanted to share it with me. Eagerly, I grabbed it from his hand and gave it a taste. When the bitter flavor exploded on my five-year-old taste buds, I spit it out then looked at him with furrowed eyebrows. "Don't ever drink this when you get older," he warned before taking back the can of beer and brown paper bag he used to conceal it. Dad knew firsthand the damaging effects alcohol could bring.

You see, alcohol runs amuck amongst the men on Dad's side. From my grandfather down, just about every male has battle scars from it. As a child, I grew to identify the smell of alcohol with Dad. Had someone asked what kind of cologne he wore, I would have said *Colt 45*, his beer of choice.

As much as I wanted him to be, Dad was not perfect. Apart from his good qualities, he had his share of faults. He was a lady's man, abused drugs and alcohol, had been to prison twice, and seemed to trust the wrong people. Unfortunately, I would meet and exceed all these things. Believe me when I say generational curses are real.

I once met a man in prison who shared a powerful story with me. Before he surrendered his life to Christ, he was an evil, mean-spirited man. Most of the respect he was given was because people feared him. His family often accused him of being just like his dad. Finally, after years of destructive behavior, he began to wonder why he was the way that he was. I was shocked when he revealed that, up to that point in his life, he had never met his dad. To me it was clear: the evil spirit that controlled his dad had controlled his life too.

Yes, generational curses are real. They will wreak havoc within families but when Christ comes onto the scene the curse can be broken.

CHAPTER THREE

PRAYER, DON'T LEAVE HOME WITHOUT IT

Two years after my parents divorced Mom remarried. She and our new stepdad began following a local televangelist and submerged themselves in his teachings. For years, we drove a total of three hours to attend weekend services. The church became their top priority and moving closer made more economic sense. Leaving friends and family behind, we moved thirty-three miles south to Akron, Ohio.

Our new residence was a three-bedroom rental house on the city's West Side. The paint chips that fell to the ground each time a storm blew in gave the house character. Most would consider it to be in the "hood", but I never saw it that way. To me it was not bad, but busy.

To keep us from being "seduced" by neighborhood kids, my siblings and I were not to play with them. It was not until we enrolled into school that I began making friends. It felt good relating to kids my age who were not my siblings. Every day I looked forward to eating lunch with them so we could share food, stories, and laughs.

Since our stepdad and mom worked, we had to walk to school. Each morning, Mom would gather us like cubs and pray for protection over us. There were times when her prayers were tested.

I was walking home from school and saw a man sitting on his porch. He was drinking from a brown paper bag, so my *Spidey Sense* was on high alert. I turned a corner and looked back, only to see the man had a gun pointed at me. Terrified, I took off running in a zigzag formation until I was far enough to feel safe. When I looked again, he was laughing hysterically. His smile vanished the moment he saw me staring. In one fluid motion, he put the brown paper bag down, grabbed the gun, and pointed it at me again. This time I did not stop running until I was home.

Another day I got caught talking and had to stay after class. Again, I was walking alone and noticed a crowd had gathered on a sidewalk and was staring at something. I crossed the street so as not to get involved. When I got directly across from them, I saw my brother lying on his back. A car, while he was trying to cross the street, had struck him. His red book bag, now several feet from his body, was as red as the blood that adorned the white snow.

A woman running toward us took my attention. It was Mom. A Good Samaritan, who went house to house searching for the child's guardian, had let her know.

The paramedics arrived and loaded him into an ambulance. Mom and I jumped in as well. He was incoherent and had a spot of blood on his head the size of a silver dollar. Thankfully, he only suffered a concussion. Today he has no effects or recollection of that incident. It is hard to tell how much God saved us from due to Mom's prayers.

As the months flew by, our involvement in the church grew rapidly. As a result, the reins became tighter on us kids. Mom and our stepdad believed in disciplining us and reinforced it with spankings. We learned fast what we could not do.

Since the rest of our family lived in Cleveland, we visited often. It just happened that Granny's home was a couple of minutes from our exit, so us asking to visit was inevitable. When allowed, our stepdad instructed us to stand at the door and to keep our coats on. If Granny did not get the hint that we would not be staying from us holding to our coats, then us huddled by her front door would drive the point home. Years later, she told me that she was privy to what was going on. She was just happy to see us, even if it was for five minutes.

Back in Akron, Mom and our stepdad struggled to make ends meet. Even with both working, making car payments, paying rent, and providing for three growing children began to take its toll.

Late one night I was in our living room and heard a commotion outside. This was normal. Our house sat beside a vacant lot and the foot traffic from short cutters was relentless. However, this noise struck me as odd. When we awakened the next morning, our car was gone and repossessed by the bank due to nonpayment. Things like this became a regular occurrence. One day the electric was off, another day the water, and so forth.

To boost morale, we decided to get a pet. Mom learned a family member was giving away a puppy and arranged to pick her up. She was so tiny that we transported her in a small paper bag. We named her Buddy.

Buddy was my best friend. She loved to sleep, play, and cuddle with me everywhere I went. We even had the same choice of toys. Let me explain.

Because she was teething, she would constantly chew on our plastic army figures. We would get after her, and she would stop for a while, but after a while she was right back at it.

One Saturday morning I stepped onto the porch to get the mail and took Buddy with me. When a kid came speeding down the street on his bike, Buddy bolted down the stairs after him. I yelled for her to return. As she did, a car came barreling down the street. I watched as it ran her over and listened to her yelp as she fought to get free from its rear tire. When she finally escaped, she came back limping, ears down, and tail between her legs.

I was hysterical. I picked her up and rushed inside the house in a panic. My brother ran into the room with a blanket, and I placed her on it. She began to shake violently as her eyes rolled to the back of her head. I tried comforting her, but she responded with a growl. This was not like her.

At once, we began to pray, believing God to heal her. Even at an early age, we knew to take our problems to Him.

As time passed the shaking stopped, but she did not move from the blanket. We kept praying. Suddenly, my brother had an idea and left the room. He returned with a tin container full of army figures. He dumped them on the floor, just out of Buddy's reach, hoping she would take the bait. She did not. We decided to leave her be but kept a close eye on her.

A couple hours later, we returned to the room and found the army figures in pieces. I had never been so excited to see our toys beheaded. We had our Buddy back! Before the day was over, her limp was completely gone, and she was back to chasing us kids around the house as if nothing had ever happened. This is the first time I remember using prayer and getting results.

Meanwhile, things were not improving for us financially. Our property owner began making house calls and brought along threats to evict us. Hearing this as a child was scary. Where would we go? How would we survive? Things like this no child should ever have to worry about. Unfortunately, I had no idea this was just the beginning of sorrows.

CHAPTER FOUR

BROKEN

After we moved, I did not see Dad as often as I would have liked. Our stepdad had major insecurities and we kids had to foot the bill. His jealousy prevented us from visiting Dad on a regular basis. As disheartening as this was, I knew Dad loved me and I loved him.

Dad was always cool as a cucumber. I don't ever recall seeing him lose his temper. However, there was an incident where I felt he came close. We were talking in Granny's living room, and I was trying to explain something to him. When I mistakenly referred to my stepdad as "my dad," I think I saw his brown eyes flicker with red. Leaning over me while pecking on his chest, he said, "Boy, I'm your daddy!" He did not raise his voice, but I knew he meant business.

Perhaps in his earlier years he would have lost it, but at this point in his life he was making moves to become a better person. One of them was enrolling into Community College. He was a loveable person with many friends. Even Granny could not deny having a soft spot for him.

Walking on Granny's grass was almost a crime, but I was not surprised to see Dad leading a game of football with his brothers and sisters in her front yard. As Granny observed from the porch, I'm sure her heart swelled with pride as she watched her kids, now grown, getting along, and having clean fun. Besides, grass is replaceable; family not so much.

It was around this time that my brother's birthdays and mine were coming up. Each year Granny would mail us kids a card with a check inside mirroring our age. This particular year she wrote a letter, asking us to call. I assumed she was planning something extra special and wanted to keep it a secret.

Since our house phone was shut off, we loaded into our new (to us) car and headed to a payphone. Mom put a quarter into the slot and dialed Granny's number. The conversation started with the usual greetings, but once the formalities were out of the way it took a tragic turn. Mom's voice seemed to have jumped two octaves. "What, Ralph's dead?" she shouted. Instantly, a wave of fear washed over me. I grabbed Mom's headrest and pulled myself up, literally sitting on the edge of my seat. *She must be talking about my grandfather, Ralph. He's much older than Dad is.*

As she gathered more information, we learned Dad was the one who had died. His best friend and next-door neighbor, while arguing about a woman, took his life from him. Dad was only thirty years old when he died from a stab wound to the chest. This occurred three days before my ninth birthday.

I was in a state of shock. My tear ducts were clogged with confusion. I didn't cry; I couldn't cry. My dad was dead. My big, strong, charismatic dad was gone. Never again would we share a hug; never again would I squeeze his muscles; never again would I hear the words, "I love you, son," come from his mouth.

The next few days were a blur. Due to the unreliability of our vehicle, a friend loaned us theirs so we could make it safely to the funeral.

The ride was unusually quiet, and everyone seemed to be in deep thought. The music, which played softly in the background, seemed to be a soundtrack to my thoughts. Our stepdad broke the silence. "You know, the day your dad died was the happiest day of my life." I was stunned. His comment did nothing but pour more fuel on the pile of questions burning in my mind. *Was Dad that bad?* The only memories I had of him were good. As I pondered his statement, he continued. "Just so you all know, we're not staying for the entire service, so sit near the back."

We arrived at the funeral home ahead of schedule. Dad's body was in a small viewing room until his service time neared. After all these years, I can close my eyes and still see him. His hair was neat, and his skin was as smooth as the suit and tie he had on. His thick mustache was well trimmed, and his lips were full just like I remembered. Had we been anywhere else, I would have thought he was sleeping.

Afraid of getting too close, I made these observations from a distance. My brother and I stood a few feet away, hugging each other, while Mom and our sister stood directly beside Dad. I wanted to cry but the dam refused to break. In a way, this was a relief. I did not want to upset our stepdad by showing emotion for Dad, so keeping it together seemed like the right thing to do.

Just before the service started, Granny came back to where we were seated. I'm sure we spoke and exchanged hugs, but I was so detached from it all that I don't remember. The only memory I have from the service is seeing my uncle on his knees, one hand on the open casket, his face buried in the other, as he sobbed uncontrollably. I wasn't used to seeing adults cry and believe this is why the memory stuck.

At home, expressing my feelings felt foreign. Saying "I love you" made me feel as if I had sucked on a lemon. We knew that we loved one another and verbalizing it did not seem necessary. Our sister, on the other hand, had no trouble expressing her feelings. Each night before bed, she would yell from her room, "Goodnight, Michael and Anthony (our brother's middle name), I love you!" This was the only time these words were uttered on a consistent basis. Mom would tell us but not nearly as much as our sister.

When Dad passed, we never spoke about it. If I could have expressed my grief verbally, it would have helped to lasso the anxiety that ran wild in my ten-year-old brain. By coping with it on my own, it set my feet on a path that would later prove to be destructive. I grew comfortable holding my emotions in when things became uncomfortable. Though it was hard to see with a naked eye, the aftermath of this tragedy birthed the first hairline crack in my foundation.

CHAPTER FIVE

FLESH DRIVEN DECISIONS

At the age of twelve I began playing the bass guitar. The first time I held it in my hands, felt the steel strings under my fingers and heard the lows rumble through the amplifier, I became obsessed. Although I am left-handed, and the guitar I borrowed was right-handed, my determination to learn outweighed the obstacle. I just turned it upside down and taught myself to play. I practiced so much that the tips of my fingers felt like I had rubbed them on hot concrete for hours, but the joy of playing overrode the pain.

Once Mom realized I was serious about it, she bought me a left-handed bass guitar. When most kids were outside playing, I was inside practicing hours at a time.

By the time I turned fourteen, my musical gifts began to flourish, and our church took notice. When they asked if I would like to volunteer in their multi-million dollar recording studio, I jumped at the opportunity.

The church also owned a TV station and had a program that

aired daily. Right away I began recording songs that went all over the world. With money coming in from across the globe, they were able to buy the best recording equipment on the market.

My working there became possible once my siblings and I started homeschooling. Eventually, they trained me to be a recording engineer, and God gave me the ability to learn at lightning speed.

Music was not the only thing that interested me. As a young, healthy, teenager, girls were beginning to register on my radar, especially one.

From the moment I laid eyes on her, I was smitten. Her long, black hair went the full length of her back, and her golden-brown skin glistened in the sun. If you can imagine Pocahontas, this was her. I pursued her for a while, and after a little cat and mouse we began to date.

Our relationship heated up when I turned sixteen. She was having trouble at home and, with no place to go, moved in with my family and me. This came as a major surprise because of how much we participated in the church, but I was not complaining. Now that we were under the same roof, we became sexually active.

With these sudden changes, I really had to double down on my double life. I had plenty of religion, but my relationship with God was nonexistent. If you read any of the Gospels (Matthew, Mark, Luke, and John), you will see just how much Jesus hated the ways of the Pharisees and Sadducees. They were hypocrites; I was a hypocrite. I went to church, shouted hallelujah, and then returned to pleasing my flesh.

Webster defines a hypocrite this way: "feigning to be what one is not or believe what one does not; the false assumption of an appearance of virtue or religion." I was the epitome of a hypocrite. It is one thing for someone to deceive you, but to deceive yourself is detrimental to one's spiritual wellbeing.

Deceit is deadly. It is like an aggressive cancer. It will eat away your soul until it is consumed (Psalm 101:7 NIV).

Pocahontas and I became inseparable. She made me feel important. When I spoke, she listened intently to every word as if I was telling her a secret. The love and attention I longed for I received from her and did not want to let it go. At age eighteen, I proposed, and she accepted.

With everything going on at work and in our relationship, I decided to drop out of high school. I never really took my education seriously and did not believe I had the skills to complete it. In my mind, I was just spinning my wheels. Unfortunately, like many of the irrational decisions I had made, this would bite me in the rear down the road.

As the wedding drew nearer, Pocahontas voiced concern. She was uncomfortable taking my last name of *Gay*, and insisted I change it before we married. I was confused but did agree to keep an open mind. Marriage is about compromise, right? Once the shock wore off, I gave it serious thought.

As a child, I admired our stepdad. During my teenage years, he was less of a parent and more like a childhood friend. My brother, our two cousins and I were video game fanatics. Instead of doing schoolwork, we all wasted countless hours on Sony's PlayStation, and our stepdad played along with us.

He had hurt his back years prior and had stopped working. He was not disabled, just deceitful and used his ailment to his advantage. On nights before his doctor's visits, he would attempt to lift our bathtub since it was not secured to the floor. This was to aggravate his back just enough to fail the exam and give him a monetary kickback from the government. We kids laughed and thought he was clever. Unfortunately, this put pressure on Mom, who was now working two jobs to support our family. For this reason, and several others, I decided to keep Dad's name.

This decision not only caused tension between Pocahontas and me, but it also put our wedding in jeopardy. For that reason, I begrudgingly agreed.

Our stepdad filed paperwork and legally adopted me, changing my last name to his by default. The shame I felt was almost too much to bear, and the disconnect I felt from my brother was immediate. I thought about the moment Dad and I shared in Granny's living room. Had he been alive, he would have *never* allowed me to change my name, regardless of how old I was. Breaking the news to Granny was gut wrenching.

In an effort to move forward, I put the anger, disappointment, and guilt I felt toward myself on my mental shelf, the same shelf I stored my feelings for losing Dad. I would deal with them later. Acting as if nothing happened seemed to work best for me, at least that is what I believed.

After saying, "I do," we moved out of my folks' place and into our own. The first few months of marriage were great. It had its challenges but nothing we could not get through with simple communication.

I was working at the church full-time, bringing home $440 every two weeks. This was barely enough to support myself, let alone my wife. The same financial rut I grew up in, I began to follow. Now the issues of money, or lack thereof, began to rear its ugly head.

I was so strapped for cash that I chose not to tithe. Malachi 3:8-11 explains God's plan of tithing. I believe this is the only time God gives us permission to test Him. By purposely disobeying

God's Word, I was sabotaging our blessings.

When the honeymoon cloud evaporated, in clear view sat a stack of bills. Suddenly our small disagreements were not so small. After falling behind on too many bills, my wife had reached her limit. I came home one day to her suggesting we move back in with my folks.

"Are you kidding me?" I objected. "I just spent eighteen years of my life with those people. There's no way I'm going back!"
She did not respond but her silence was deafening.

Finally, after a few weeks of stress, and against my better judgment, we moved back in with my folks.

CHAPTER SIX

BETRAYED

During the time we were out of the house, my stepdad started working. My wife needed a better paying job, and he got her hired at his location.

I was still working for the church, and my load steadily increased. I even began bringing projects home. The creative engine in my mind ran continuously, and I did not know how to channel it into other areas of my life. I became so involved that I began to neglect my wife, and our marriage began to suffer.

When I finally realized the error of my ways, the tide had already shifted and was gaining strength in the wrong direction. I expressed that my ignoring her was done in ignorance, but it fell on deaf ears. The gulf that separated us seemed too big to mend. Even while in the same room, we were miles apart. Naturally, this had a negative impact on our intimacy. She spurned my advances and was overly cold. It was so extreme that I suspected her of cheating, but all she did was work and then return home.

I reverted to some of the things I did when we dated but nothing mattered. All the hope I had of saving our marriage was gone. I did not want anyone to know our marriage was on life-support, so I refused to talk with anyone. Pride is a powerful tool the enemy uses on us (Proverbs 29:23).

As things worsened, the more I felt like a cheap balloon at maximum capacity. Something had to give, or I was subject to burst at any time. To alleviate stress, I adopted a method called pain transference. Whenever I was overwhelmed, I would take a sharp object and cut myself. This is not of God. Scripture tells us that Legion would cut himself before Jesus cast the impure spirits out of him (Mark 5:5).

I kept this ritual a secret. The only person close enough to notice the scars was my wife, but the distance between us, both emotional and physical, prevented that from happening. Unless she is reading this, she still does not know.

I did not realize it then, but the devil had me right where he wanted. Alone. Had I been in my right mind, I would have sought godly counsel (Proverbs 11:14).

Things finally hit the fan when I spoke to our pastor who was also my boss. We talked about work until he asked about my marriage. That was when I voiced my concerns. He seemed to have taken them to heart and offered to speak to her, which gave me hope.

As I waited backstage to perform, I saw my wife enter the pastor's office. Knowing so much hinged on this meeting, I took to the stage physically weak and stressed. As I played my guitar, one of the cuts on my wrist opened. I sighed, remembering I had a way to alleviate the stress. It would be an intense cutting session, but I was willing to do whatever it took to escape.

Unfortunately, it would have to wait because the pastor summoned me to his office. Having grown up in the church, and being incredibly ornery, I had been to his office multiple times. Normally, he stood in front of his desk, but this time he was pacing. When I closed the door, he did not hold back.

"Well, son, your suspicions were right. Your wife confessed to having an affair with your stepdad..." BOOM! Just like that, my life was in shambles. Everything else he said was irrelevant. All I could do was shake my head in disbelief. I started to remove my wedding ring when he raised his hand in objection. "No, No, don't do that," he ordered. "I don't want them to know that you know just yet."

I stood there befuddled. His voice trailed off as my thoughts took precedence. *You just dropped a mental bomb on me and you're telling me to act as if nothing's wrong??No problem. I've done this my entire life.*

His voice returned to full volume. I secured the ring on my finger, thanked him for getting to the truth, and left his office. Walking to my car on nothing but adrenaline I headed home, the same home where my wife and stepdad would be.

I held it together in the office, but inside I seethed with anger. My mind was stuck in a swirling eddy, so I took the long way, driving slowly to gather my thoughts.

I gripped the steering wheel even tighter as I thought of my stepdad, the man who practically raised me and the man whose last name I now carried. I hated him! Not only did he ruin my life, my mom's and siblings' lives would change too. I no longer wanted to cut myself; I wanted to cut him!

I turned onto our street, shutoff my headlights and coasted to a parking spot in front of the house. I exited the car and used a streetlight behind me, and the driver's side window to straighten my bowtie. With guitar in hand, I looked at the house and released another deep sight. "Well, here goes nothing," I mumbled with little confidence. I walked to the door, put the key into the lock, and mustered the best poker face I could.

CHAPTER SEVEN

SUFFERING IN SILENCE

The house was unusually dark. Ordinarily, after a Sunday night service, there would be at least one person watching TV, but that was not the case. I knew from this slight change in routine that my wife's confession was out. I also realized Mom did not know because, if she did, lights would have been on and conversations would have been had.

Slowly, I opened the door, unsure of what to expect. With stealth like agility, I made my way to my room, changed out of my tuxedo, and got into bed. On this night, the Sandman and I would be enemies. I would not sleep a wink.

It was a few days until Mom learned what had happened. Although she handled it better than I did, she was still crushed. On one occasion, I witnessed her crumble to the floor under the weight of it all. So many times, I wished her pain on me. I loved her too much to watch her suffer. Had I the power, I would have taken her hurt.

This is what Jesus wants to do for us. He promised to give us peace in exchange for our burdens (Matthew 11:28). He knows our limitations and is willing and able to do for us that which we cannot do for ourselves. We have nothing to lose by trusting in Him. I did not realize this at the time and was determined to maintain control of my life.

After eighteen years of marriage, Mom filed for divorce and never looked back. Each time we spoke, she made it clear that there was no chance of reconciliation. I, on the other hand, driven by hate for my stepdad, decided to work things out with my wife. Don't get me wrong, I still loved my wife, but more than anything I believed walking away would mean he had won. I refused to let that happen.

This type of thinking and pride dominated my life. The optimism I once had for a successful marriage quickly became an obsession. I was suspicious of everything. If she came home with a shoe untied, I wanted an explanation.

Some of my friends tried talking sense into me but I did not want to hear it. To keep them and everyone else off my back, I decided to suffer in silence. Some days were harder than others, but I stood firm on my decision. At the heart of it all, losing Dad made me fearful of losing anyone close to me. As a result, I became super possessive and attached.

My brother, who is a man of few words, told me that I was not the same Michael from years past. This bothered me because I knew there was some validity to his statement. Deep within, I knew I was losing myself but refused to reach for help. His comment also made me realize I was slipping and needed to tighten up. If he noticed something was off, others would too. After all, I had an image to maintain.

I have always been quick witted and at the time believed my tongue was my strongest weapon. Before I knew it, I was verbally abusing my wife. At some point, talking no longer had an effect, and I figured I could show her better than I could tell her.

One Sunday afternoon, during an intense argument, I lost control of my temper and shoved her to the floor. It happened so fast that it scared me. I can only imagine how she felt. Ten minutes later, I was sitting in the back of a police car. This was my first encounter with the law.

On the way to the station, I told the arresting officer what had led to my arrest. The more I talked, the better I felt. Opening to a stranger was unlike me, but it was a clear indication of how much I was holding in.

The officer listened without interrupting and then offered some advice. "If something like this ever happens again, walk away and don't come back until you've cleared your head. That's what I do when my wife and I get into it. Believe me, it's not worth it."

Just when I was beginning to like the guy, he said something stupid like this. There was no way I was going to roll over and go belly-up. I ignored the fact I had done so many times before, all for the wrong reasons. The punishment for this first-time offense was thirty days of house arrest. For whatever reason, they allowed me to serve it at home with my wife. Makes sense, right?

After completing the thirty days, I moved out. We were still sleeping together, but I needed space.

To keep my mind busy, I dove headfirst into work. No matter what was going on around me, I found peace in music. I worked a lot of overtime and kept busy in other ways; but, after a couple of months, I found myself missing my wife.

Our well-respected pastor at the time lost all respect for my wife after she confessed. He let me know that if I went back to her, I would be putting my job in jeopardy.

In order to stay out of sight, I snuck around to see her. (As I write this, I realize how crazy this sounds but it's what I did). We would be intimate in secret, and I would shun her in public. She did not deserve that.

Our church made it clear they were only interested in helping me and ostracized her. I thought the role of a church was to help the broken. Perhaps I got a free pass because I was of some value to them.

Eventually, our pastor learned I had not heeded his warning. He pulled me into his office and told me that, if I disobeyed him again, not only would he fire me, but God would disown me.

Digesting this was painful. I was already battling issues of acceptance. Hearing I was one decision away from God rejecting me as mind shattering. That day my view of God changed. I believed, regardless of what I did, He was angry at me. Moving forward, I just did the best I could on my own.

Not long after this scolding, our church began to prepare for a missionary trip to South Africa. I received news that I would be working at the services. On top of that, I also learned my wife was pregnant. I had mixed feelings; I did not like the fact I was sneaking around to see her and felt pressured on every side.

For the first time in a long time, I spoke a prayer of sincerity, hoping God would understand why I felt this way. Deep inside, I did not think He cared. If "God's mouthpiece" said I was just about doomed for hell, then there was nothing more I could do.

CHAPTER EIGHT

LOVE, GOD'S UNIVERSAL LANGUAGE

2005 was a year of many firsts. It would be my first missionary trip and my first time flying in an airplane. It would also be the first time I had been away from my wife for more than a couple of days. Our fifteen days apart would set a record.

Saying goodbye proved to be more difficult than expected. My issues of trust, or lack thereof, beat me up day and night. There was no way I would get a handle on it before I left, so I forced myself to shelve it or risk ruining the trip.

Our church was also experiencing a first. It would be the first time their newly purchased Boeing 747 jet went into use. To put the icing on the cake, the church's restaurant would be catering a portion of the food. I had heard stories from those who had flown before, and what I was walking into was like nothing they had ever experienced. With about ninety of us flying, the plane was nowhere near capacity. This gave us ample room to spread out.

After the eighteen-hour flight, plus the hour it took to refuel, we landed in South Africa. The beauty of this continent was amazing, and the smiles that greeted us were as warm as the midday sun. Many of the airport staff were awestruck by the size of our plane. Some had even come aboard to view it.

Once we disembarked, we headed for Customs. The plan was for everyone to stick together until all had gone through. Each person filed through the line, but things slowed when my turn came. One worker manned the computer while another came over and went through my suitcase. Evidently, my run-in with the law flagged me in their system. Thankfully, it was only a misdemeanor, or our twenty-minute delay could have been worse.

Waiting outside was a tour bus that would taxi us to our hotel. As we drove along, I took in the culture of the African people.

One of the first things I noticed was the pungent odor of something burning. As I tried to discern the smell, a woman walking toward us caught my eye. Both hands were full of bags and there was a plastic container on her head balanced to perfection. Just as we were about to pass her, I turned and saw a baby strapped to her back. I grinned. The baby did not appear to have a care in the world. I would learn over the next two weeks just how resilient the African people are.

The deeper we went into the city, the more things went from pretty to poverty. Images I had only seen on TV commercials stared me in the face. Seeing kids with tattered clothes, frail bodies, living in dilapidated shanties hurt my soul. *God, please help them,* I prayed as tears dripped from my eyes.

So many things I had complained about seemed trivial compared to their needs. Even as a child, my family's lowest moment would have been their dream. Yes, there were times when we could not afford food, or needed clothing and money; but, when we could not get those things, our government helped.

We arrived at the hotel, and I helped unload the luggage. When I grabbed mine, it seemed heavier than I remembered. The guilt I carried knowing I would be sleeping in a warm, cozy room seemed to add weight not only to my luggage but to my heart as well.

Africa was in the midst of winter when we arrived. Although the days were hot, the nights were chilly. It just did not feel right knowing some of my African brothers and sisters would be out in the elements. Regardless of age, color, and location, we all need the same necessities of life.

The next morning the crew and I went to a soccer field and setup for the upcoming services. As we approached the field, the same burning odor bombarded my nose. I exited the van and scattered on the ground were the remains of discolored corncobs. I would learn that the locals loved to grill corn and eat it like apples. To me, the smell was putrid. I grew to have a love and hate relationship with corn on the cob while there.

We unloaded our truck and began to setup when three local boys, ages eight, ten, and thirteen, approached our supervisor and asked to help. He agreed and we worked side by side until it was time for lunch. The supervisor gave the young men money to buy food, while the crew and I reconvened underneath the stage we had built to hide from the scorching sun. Before I unpacked my lunch, I cleaned my hands with sanitizer I had brought just as our helpers returned with their food. I nibbled on my sandwich but was far more interested in what they were doing.

All three of them roamed the field, appearing to be looking for something on the ground. Suddenly, the eight-year-old stooped and wiggled his hands in a muddy puddle the rain had birthed the night before. This was how all of them cleaned his hands.

Next, the oldest sat the two younger boys down and then opened the boxed chicken dinner. He took out a biscuit, fed a bite to the youngest, and then gave a bite to the other, before finally taking a bite for himself. I had never seen anything like this.

On another occasion, we had just finished a long day of setting up. I grabbed my belongings and headed to the van. I did not get far before a young man stopped me.

"Suh, may I have your wah-tuh?" he said in broken English. The water in that area was not good, so we brought some with us.

Behind him were about twenty-five other men who were building a rock wall. It may have been a work requirement, or perhaps a punishment, but each of them wore matching jumpsuits.

"I'm sorry," I explained, "but I can't give it to you because I don't have enough for everyone." He tucked his head, and replied, "I understand," before walking away. I stood there, unsure of what to do but knew I had to do something. I was worn out from the long day, and they were still going.

"Hey!" I shouted, "It's yours!" I tossed the water into the air, and he caught it as if it were the winning catch in game seven of a World Series. Had it slipped through his fingers, I am confident his large smile would have caught it.

When the other men saw he had water, they jumped off the wall, surrounded him, and began to dance and sing as he poured water into each of their mouths. This was an unforgettable moment.

Our purpose for being there was to share the love of Christ.

Many of them were open to hearing the Good News and some had even repented of their sins and accepted Jesus on the spot. It was an amazing experience, not just for them but for me as well.

The highlight of the trip came when I visited a hospital and ministered to the sick. From their malnourished bodies to the abhorrent smell in the air, I knew Death was waiting to claim its next victim. Some lay dying with AIDS and I was able to offer them eternal life, the same eternal life Jesus spoke of in John 11:25.

I was not afraid to touch them; I was doing the Lord's work. I am sure they felt like outcasts. Not only did they *need* to know they were loved, but they needed to *feel* loved as well.

We are no different from them. Their illness manifested externally while many of our issues lie internally. One of the good things about God is He does not focus on what we look like on the outside. He's more concerned about the status of our heart (1 Samuel 16:7).

Our time there had come to an end and, as I stepped out of the room, a woman holding a baby approached me requesting prayer. While we stood in the lobby, I closed my eyes and began to pray. In Mark16:17,18, Jesus instructs believers to lay hands on the sick and they will recover. When I opened my eyes to lay hands on the baby, women stretching their babies toward me, desperate to have their child prayed over, surrounded me.

I was already on the verge of tears, and this moment broke me. So many of these women were sick and no doubt dying, and the only thing they wanted was a blessing for their child. There is nothing like the love of a mother. Before we left, I prayed over every baby and mother present. That was the moment I knew a part of my heart would remain in South Africa.

God met many needs that day. Not because of me, it happened

because they used their faith, just like the woman in Mark 5:25-34 who had a blood disease and needed healing. She had suffered for twelve long years and spent every dime she had on doctors, only to be in a worse condition. She knew about Jesus and heard He would be passing through her town. With her mind made up, she knew that, if she could just get close enough to touch His robe, her healing would come. Already weak from loss of blood, she joined the crowd and used every ounce of strength she could muster to get to The Master.

Finally, Jesus arrived full of power and overflowing with compassion. As she fell to the ground from exhaustion, she reached out and touched His robe, and the flow of blood stopped immediately.

Jesus, realizing healing power had left His body, turned, and asked, "Who touched Me?" Perplexed by the enquiry, His disciples said, "How can you ask such a thing? These people are grasping at you from every direction!" Nevertheless, Jesus knew this touch was different.

A hush came over the crowd as Jesus looked around. The woman, now trembling from fear, came forward and bowed at His feet, confessing to what she had done. Feeling ashamed, she would not look Him in the face. But Jesus, moved with compassion, gently lifted her head by the chin, and said, "Daughter, be of good cheer. Your faith has made you well. Go in peace. You won't suffer anymore."

The lesson here is a lesson of faith. Our faith in God gets His attention. He is drawn to faith as a moth is to a flame. Our job is to believe, and God will do the rest.

I can honestly say that I have never seen love like the love I saw in South Africa. It's a shame I had to travel over a thousand miles to see it.

Leaving would be bittersweet. I fell in love with the African people but was starting to get homesick.

The day before we left, we took a tour of the city. While walking, I met a sixty-year-old woman who was selling handmade sculptures. One item caught my eye. It was a large piece of wood, shaped into the continent of Africa with hippos, elephants, and other exotic creatures on it. Whatever she was asking did not matter. I had to have it. That year, one American dollar was equivalent to fourteen of their dollars, or Rand. She gave me her price, which I felt was low, so I planned to give her a little extra. When I reached for my money, I was out of Rand. Without hesitating, I handed her a crisp $20 bill. I did not think much of it. I was just excited to take her creation home.

When the woman received the money, she went bonkers! She jumped up and down with excitement and then her joy turned into tears of gratitude. "God bless you! God bless you!" she cried. "Your mother did a good job raising you!" It was not until the plane ride home that I realized I had given her $280 in her money. I smiled. Her reaction let me know she was in great need. The extra I was going to give her would have been nice, but God had bigger plans.

You cannot put a dollar amount on something as precious as this. There is so much more joy in *giving* than there is in receiving. That dear woman has remained in my heart all these years. I hope to see her in heaven one day.

May God bless the African people and all who are suffering around the world.

CHAPTER NINE

THE COST OF SUFFERING IN SILENCE

Shortly after returning home, I received a call that my wife had gone into labor. Not wanting to expose myself to the sneaking around I was doing, I remained at work when she gave birth to our daughter. I did go to the hospital the following day, but it was not the same. When my wife and daughter needed me the most, I was not there. I was already a crummy husband, and my first few hours as a dad were not very impressive.

As I held our baby in my arms, her beauty hypnotized me. She had her mom's hair, and from the way she gripped my finger she had my strength. The weight of responsibility bore down on me as I stared into her innocent eyes. I knew she needed raised in the ways of the Lord, but it would be impossible to do in my current state.

It was not long until I learned the affair between my wife and stepdad never ended, even while I was in Africa. It felt like every moment my wife and I shared was a lie. Having to relive the hurt and humiliation was too much and choosing to suffer in silence had taken its toll.

I had never faced depression, but it hit me like a ton of bricks. Unbeknownst to me, the spirit of depression runs deep within Mom's family. In fact, one of her relatives killed herself while battling it. I had seen traces of it in Mom but had never experienced it directly. I did not even know I was depressed, but I did notice how sad I was all the time.

One summer day, I was driving across a bridge and heard a voice say, "You should kill yourself right here!" The eerie voice sent chills throughout my body. It startled me but not as much as it should have. My choosing to suffer in silence had prepared me for this moment, and the devil had me right where he wanted me, alone, confused, and broken.

Looking back, I can see Satan's tactics with greater clarity. If he can get us far enough from God, he will have a better chance at capturing us than if we were to stay by God's side. Not many people realize how patient the enemy is. Sometimes he will wait years until the gap between us and God is large enough for him to attack.

Before I cleared the bridge I agreed with the voice. Life is a precious gift, and I felt unworthy of it. The enemy kept feeding my depressed mind thoughts of how the world would be better without me in it, and I gobbled them whole.

I pulled off the bridge, parked my car, and started to walk. What's crazy is at the time I was afraid of heights. Psychologically, I knew what I was doing; physically, I had no control over my body. It was as if an unseen force was controlling me. When I was finally able to stop, I looked over the rail and found myself at the peak of the bridge. I stood motionless, frozen in fear when an ambulance drove up.

"Are you okay?" the passenger shouted. His voice snapped me out of whatever mindset I was in.

"Yes, I'm fine. Just going for a walk," I replied, flashing a false smile. Satisfied with my response, they drove away.

I believe God sent that ambulance to get my attention. Had He not, I don't think I would be here today.

If you are reading this and have been contemplating suicide, reading this is not a coincidence. God sent me to get your attention. Whatever problem you are facing, God has a promise, a solution for it in His Word. In your brokenness, tell the Lord how you feel. Tell Him that you cannot live this life on your own and need His help. Ask Him to take away those evil thoughts and to replace them with His peace, joy, and love. He *will* do it! Only believe. Others may have let you down, but God will *NEVER* let you down.

With the fog dissipating from my mind, I did not trust myself to walk to my car. I called my brother and told him everything. From there, I spent the next three days in a psychiatric unit. When Mom came to visit, I was upset about being there.

"Mom," I whined, "look around. *These* people are crazy. I don't need to be here!" To which she replied, "No, Michael, you need help!"

To confirm her statement, after my release, I continued playing house with my wife. When arguments got out of hand, the calls to the cops increased, as did the misdemeanors on my record.

Eventually, my wife went to a courthouse and got an order of protection. That set me off even more. I was not going to let a judge tell me what I could not do. This stubbornness landed me in court several times for violating that order. The next charge would be a felony, which meant possible time in prison.

But, I still rode the fence. I knew how far to take things without crossing the line. I also had one of the best defense lawyers in our region.

I was a loose cannon. All the while, God continued to flash warning signs along my path to help me avoid what was ahead. STOP, DANGER, ROAD CLOSED, DETOUR, and YIELD, were some of the signs I ignored.

He also sent people with words of wisdom, but it went in one ear and out the other. Even Granny weighed in.

"You see, the court is making you do what you should've done all along, walk away."
Yeah... I hear you, Grandma."

There was one conversation Granny and I had that put things into perspective. What she said was simple yet profound. "Grandson, you can't make someone love you."

Out of everything I had gone through with my wife, at the end of the day I just wanted her to love me. My obsessive behavior was my way of forcing her to do so. I never shared this with Granny. The Spirit of God put those words in her mouth.

After several years of fighting, I finally raised my white flag and took my losses. Shortly thereafter, we divorced.

CHAPTER TEN

MY WILL BE DONE

Things were much better now that I was divorced. Although the pastor terminated me, I found a good paying construction job.

After a few months of the single life, I began going to clubs and took my first drink at age twenty-four (excluding the drink Dad gave me at age five). My friends were shocked at how much I could drink and still function. I attribute this to the alcohol abuse in my family.

I had never done drugs and did them need to. Partying became a drug. I lived for it on the weekends and the women that came with it. Regardless of how confident I came across, my self-esteem issues were always at the forefront of my mind.

Over the years, I had developed a personal vendetta toward women. I never got over what my ex-wife did to me. I also never forgot Dad's murder was about a woman. Any woman that I met already had two strikes against them. All the unresolved issues I thought I had buried had shaped me into an inconsiderate idiot.

One night I met a gorgeous blonde-haired woman. We were spending time together when she asked if I had ever done cocaine. Before I could answer, she uncovered a heart shaped mirror with cocaine on it and started breaking it into lines. I had never seen cocaine in person and felt uneasy with it in front of me.

"Naw, I'm good," I replied, weakly, then she laughed.

"Did you think I wanted you to do all of this? Here... just try a little," she instructed, sliding the mirror toward me. I felt my manhood was under attack and my pride would not let that ride. I picked up the straw and inhaled as hard as I could. Had I known how much that little bump would change my life, I would have run for my life.

From that moment forward I was hooked. The day I met with a dealer, I thought I bought cocaine. In hindsight, cocaine bought me. Everything in my life began to center on getting high. Unlike the marijuana I had tried months earlier, I could function on cocaine.

By nature I am a social butterfly, but using cocaine took me to inconceivable heights. As the saying goes, "The higher you climb, the harder you fall."

The life that comes from being a drug addict changed me into the exact person I despised, a liar. According to a good friend, I was now "user friendly." In other words, once I got what I needed from you, I would disappear until I needed you again.

Although I was making good money as a construction worker, it was not something I was passionate about. My heart was still in music, so it only made sense to pursue it.

I searched all over for recording studios in my area but found nothing worth leaving my stable job. I decided to search out of state and took interest in a recording studio in Manhattan, New York.

I reached out and made a solid connection with an employee. We stayed in contact, and I eventually landed an interview.

On a brisk, snowy, November night, I made the nine-hour, white knuckle drive to Manhattan. I was exhausted and used the six hours until the interview to get some shuteye. I awakened refreshed and went looking for the studio. Unbeknownst to me, the GPS did not factor in the construction detours. I found myself driving down a four lane, one-way street, and in the wrong direction. Thankfully, a few bystanders let me know in good ole New York fashion that I needed to turn around immediately.

I located the building and expected to see something spectacular, not a plain, drab, high-rise. My initial thought was I had made a mistake. That changed when I entered the door of their suite.

Adorned on the walls were gold and platinum albums from legendary artists like Run DMC, superstar Mya, and many others. There were also awards for soundtrack recordings to movies like Shrek, American Gangster, and many more. Singer John Legend frequented the studio, and *Good Morning America* conducted an interview with pop star Justin Bieber in the very lobby in which I stood.

Before I drowned in drool, an employee came out and greeted me. He would give me a tour until the manager was available. The first room we entered was Studio A, their main recording studio.

"We just purchased this recording console from the Saturday

Night Live set a few weeks ago. You can buy one for about six figures, if you're interested," he teased.

I spun around and felt like a kid in a candy store while looking at the equipment. Everything was pristine.

When the manager joined, I felt overdressed. His simple jeans and tee made my dress shoes and button-down shirt seem like I was going to a church revival. The two of us continued the tour and then got down to business.

First, he went over the ground rules. "A lot of celebrities come here," he said, "and it's unprofessional to ask for their autograph. They are here to work, not perform. Once you've developed a relationship with them then that's different. We try to keep them away from the groupies as much as possible."

"Understood," I answered.

He smiled. "Good. One of the perks of working here is we attend the Grammy's each year, so you'll have that to look forward to."

I kept composure, but my excitement was growing.

He paused and then looked at my resume. "What is it you want to do here?" I was perplexed by his question. I thought I had made it clear what my intentions were.

"Sir, I'm interested in the recording engineer position. I want to record the talent that comes in."

"I get that, but I heard you play bass. If I need you to record bass on someone's album, I want you to be open to doing it. Don't sell yourself short… So how soon can you start?"

I could not believe my ears. This was a dream come true. I did my best to match his demeanor. "The first of the year would be best. That's all the time I need to get my affairs in order."

"Great!" he said, shaking my hand.

I waited to return home before sharing the news with Mom who was equally excited. I did not have much confidence, but one thing I knew was God had gifted me in music.

As I finalized my plans, the thought of leaving my daughter stopped me in my tracks. I never considered how my decision to leave would affect her. The closer I came to the move date, the more her beautiful face flashed before me. I concluded that moving was to give her a better life, but the guilt remained.

A few weeks before moving to the Big Apple, I spent the day with some friends. It was a call I received there that changed everything.

CHAPTER ELEVEN

ROTTEN APPLES

On the other end of the phone was a detective. His thick, raspy voice indicated he was in no mood to play.

"Hi, this is Detective Ruff. Do you know why I'm calling you?"

"No, I don't."

"You don't know why I'm calling you?" he said, growing annoyed.

"Sir, I have no idea!"

"I'm calling because you violated your protection order.

"No, I didn't."

"Yes, you did! We're typing a warrant for your arrest and will see you soon!" CLICK!

Here's the thing: since my divorce, I had not spoken to my ex-wife. Why the cop called was a mystery. I thought it was a prank until Detective Ruff called again.

"I was reviewing your file and noticed that you're looking at a felony. Are you willing to come to the station and give us a statement?"

"Why, so you can arrest me? I don't think so!" I ended the call.

I was in a daze. I explained to my friend what had happened, and we drove to a Verizon Wireless store. We spoke to a manager who confirmed I had not placed any calls to my ex-wife.

Knowing my arrest was imminent, I decided to lay low. Eventually, I hired an attorney and turned myself in with him present.

That day the courtroom was packed and had pockets of chatter within the crowd. I was the first person called. I stood before the judge more anxious than nervous, wondering why I was there in the first place. The prosecutor must have poured Red Bull in his espresso and watched one too many episodes of Judge Judy because his performance was camera worthy.

"Your Honor," he shouted while pointing, "This man won't leave this woman alone!" The judge heard my snicker on the microphone and showed his displeasure with a stern look atop his glasses. The prosecutor, whose antics now silenced the courtroom, was on a roll.

"Your Honor, the defendant has been harassing this woman. He's called her multiple times and even left a voicemail that said, *&%$, you're dead!"

Now I wasn't laughing. With those kinds of accusations, there was no way I would walk out a free man. I knew I was innocent, but how could I explain something I did not even understand? Fortunately, I would have time to ponder the thought because the judge sent me to jail. Of all the terrible things I had done, I was being punished for something I did *not* do.

I sat on a bunk wondering whom to turn to for help. My addiction had turned me into a liar, and I did not think anyone believed I was telling the truth.

I got to know my bunkmate (bunkie) and shared the details of my case, proclaiming my innocence. After the second day, I stopped talking because just about everyone claimed to be innocent.

My back was against a wall. God was my only hope. He knew the truth, and only He could reveal it. At wits end, I promised God that I would get my life together if He would uncover the truth (many promises are made to God while incarcerated).

One week later, I returned to court. When my attorney presented my phone records he had subpoenaed to prove my innocence, the prosecutor objected, "Your Honor, how do we know these records aren't fabricated?"

Just when I thought things could not get any worse, they did when the police officer took the stand. "Your Honor, I actually spoke to him! I was taking his ex-wife's statement, and when he called, she handed me the phone."

I slumped even lower in my chair. None of this made any sense. The only thing I could conjure up was the police officer and my ex-wife were an item and wanted me out the picture. Even then, why bother me if I was not bothering them?

The judge was torn but took the officer's side and sent me back to jail. Seeing the disappointment on Mom's face as I exited in handcuffs was heartbreaking.

After my second week in jail, Granny and a friend made the two-hour drive and bonded me out. She was always coming to my rescue, and I relied more on her than I relied on God, but He would fix that soon enough.

Three months had passed, and I was back in court ready to fight my case. As I entered the lobby, my attorney exited the courtroom, smiling ear to ear. "Case dismissed,"

"What do you mean?" I countered.

"The prosecutor traced the alleged call you made to your stepdad's computer. He used a program to call your ex-wife and put in your number. The third-degree felony you were going to get, the State has given to him. What's more, the judge ordered him to pay you the $1,750 you spent to hire me, along with your court fees."

I could not believe my ears. God had done it! He uncovered everything!

I did not know how big the case was until it made the local newspaper. When everything ended, the entire incident was expunged from my record. It is as if it never happened. Unfortunately, while the wrinkles were ironed out in the case, I was not allowed to leave Ohio, thus losing the job in New York.

In life, there are things we will never understand. Could I have avoided all of this had I sought God's will in moving to New York? Only He knows. What I do know is He rescued me when I reached out to Him. If He heard my prayers, He will hear yours too.

CHAPTER TWELVE

GOD, I'M BUSY, LEAVE A MESSAGE

Up until that point in my life God had never moved in such a personal and powerful way. He did everything His Word said He would do. Now I had to hold up my end of the deal. I just needed to take care of a few things first.

This case had tarnished my reputation, and what others thought about me mattered a lot. They needed to know I was telling the truth all along and could be trusted. This would have been the perfect opportunity to share how God exonerated me, but that would have to wait. It was my time to shine underneath the spotlight.

I once heard someone say, "God is willing to share His heaven with us; He is willing to share His power with us; He is even willing to share His Son with us, but the one thing He will never share is His glory." In my quest to look good, I was in essence stealing God's glory, and there was no way He would let that fly.

When my friends learned my case had been overturned, they wanted to celebrate. (Honestly, I could have told them I ate all my veggies at lunch, and they would have found a reason to celebrate, just so it included alcohol.)

The same day God gave me another chance at life, I repaid Him by getting sloppy drunk before the night was over. It was only three months before that I was on my knees, begging Him to keep me from going to prison. I may have been able to fool those around me, but I would never fool God. Galatians 6:7 (ERV) says, *if you think you can fool God, you are only fooling yourselves. You will harvest what you plant.*

Just because the consequences of our sins are not dealt out immediately, we may think God does not care, but He does. He never turns a blind eye to sin. Proverbs 15:3 tells us *The eyes of the Lord are in every place, keeping watch on the evil and the good.*

Imagine you had a job that paid daily, but instead of cashing the checks you held on to them. After a while, the checks would pile up. However, once they are cashed, you'll be in for a huge payday.

In the same way, this is what happens when we sin and fail to repent. It is like storing checks. When payday comes, it won't be pleasant. Romans 6:23 (ERV) says, *When people sin, they earn what sin pays - death. But God gives his people a free gift - eternal life in Christ Jesus our Lord.*

Sin is a big deal to God, so big that He sent His only Son to die in our place for sins He would never commit. Sometimes we find it hard to be nice to a person who cuts us off in traffic, spreads rumors about us, or wrongs us in other ways. We would never die for them, but Jesus did. Romans 5:7,8 (ERV) reads, *Very few people will die to save the life of someone else, even if it is for a good person. Someone might be willing to die for an especially good person. But Christ died for us while we were still sinners, and by this God showed how much He loves us.*

Now that I was drinking again, it did not take long for me to resume using drugs. I still planned to keep the promise I made to God, but I would dictate the time. That's how warped my mind had become. I thought I could tell Almighty God, ruler of heaven and earth, The Creator, when I was ready to come home. I was deceived on so many levels. Jesus said, *No one can come to Me unless the Father who sent Me draws him* (John 6:44).

God's plan of salvation is simple. It is so simple that we often complicate it. He laid it out in such a way that we would have nothing to do with it. If we did, we might boast about what we did to receive it and steal God's glory (Ephesians 2:8,9).

The truth of the matter is this: Jesus shed His blood so we could be forgiven from our sins (Hebrews 9:22), the Holy Spirit convicts us of sin (John 16:8) and gives us a desire to be saved. God is the One who gives us faith to believe in Him, and "If we confess our sins, He is faithful and just to forgive us our sins and to cleanse us from all unrighteousness" (1 John 1:9).

Despite my reckless thinking, God would not let up. His Spirit followed me into bars, dope houses, strip clubs, and every other ungodly place I stepped foot in. He pursued me like I had something He wanted, and He did - my heart. He was after my heart. Not just a part of it but the whole thing. That day at Calvary, Jesus paid a hefty price for me and was ready to collect on His investment.

I ran for as long as I could away from His convicting presence but outrunning Him was something I could not do. Just below the surface was a God-shaped hole in my heart, which slowed my pace. A spiritual heart-murmur. We are all born with this defect. We spend so much of our lives trying to fill this void with earthly things when only Christ can fill it.

My life was running off the rails. I had an amazing poker face and could hide behind a smile, but I was stuffing so much inside that I began to come apart at the seams. The emotional trauma I harbored through the years was eating me alive. I could conceal it while sober, but when I drank it would seep out, making me an emotional mess.

On those inebriated nights, my friends would tell me the next day that I had been crying about my dad. I would spin it as if it were no big deal, but deep inside I was hemorrhaging from hurt.

I missed Dad terribly and had so any questions, questions about his death but more about his life. There was so much I did not know, like, what made him happy? What traits did we share? What really happened the night he died? These thoughts tormented me, and I sensed a breakdown coming.

Usually when I felt this way, I would drop everything and visit Granny. God's peace rested in her home, and the public anointing she carried was a result of everything she did in private.

2 Corinthians 3:17 (NIV) says, *And where the Spirit of the Lord is, there is freedom.* The God-shaped hole in my heart identified with the presence of the Lord in her home. My soul craved it, but I wanted it on my terms.

Oftentimes, I would show-up unannounced to surprise her. A few of those times it backfired, and I was left sitting on the steps of her porch. However, on this trip I was successful.

I arrived at her home, and we greeted each other with a heartfelt hug, as was the norm. We sat on a sofa and caught up as my uncle entered through the front door. He took a seat beside Granny and joined the conversation. I could not help but think of Dad. I imagined how awesome it would have been if he were with us.

I would have the same thoughts at our family gatherings. Usually, I was the talker in the bunch; but, when someone mentioned Dad's name, I would fall back and listen to whatever stories they wanted to share. Those were special moments.

As we talked on the sofa, my uncle's jubilant demeanor fell flat when I asked him to share a few things about Dad. I felt guilty for putting him in that predicament and did my best not to ask any more questions.

In an effort to feel closer to Dad, I began hanging with my uncle when I shouldn't have. These were the years in his life when he was battling a lot of demons. Now in his late forties, the drug and alcohol addiction which began when he was thirteen years old was consuming his life (I say *was* because at the time of this writing, he is six years sober!) Smoking crack and drinking alcohol were his drugs of choice.

My uncle's addictions aside, he was an extremely thoughtful, funny, and hardworking man. When it came to Granny, he always showed her respect. Known for being a straight shooter, if you did not want to know the truth about yourself, you had better cross the street if you saw him coming. I have no recollection of Dad's smile, but if it was anything like my uncle's then it was nothing short of amazing.

At the time, my uncle lived in a house directly in front of Granny's home. One day I walked over, and he was in the basement. After a few minutes of talking, he pulled out a crackpipe and lit it up. I had my reservations, and rightfully so, but figured compromising a little would strengthen our relationship. I took a puff, but it did not hit me the way I expected. I took another puff and then gave up.

Still feeling *normal*, I returned to Granny's home, but things changed. She was sitting at the table, so I made sure to keep my distance to keep her from smelling my smoke laced clothes. All it took was a glance for her to say, "Boy, you look like you got into something that you know you shouldn't have!" I did not have my wits about me to deny it, so I went back to my uncle's until it wore off.

At Granny's home, there was no need to set an alarm. The smell of eggs, bacon, grits, and toast was how I was used to waking up, and the next day was no different. If I wanted a hot meal, I knew to go downstairs before it got cold because she was not waking me up.

From the time I was a child, Granny always made me a plate and set it on the table next to a cold glass of orange juice. She would always say, "Alright, Grandson, turn that TV off and come eat." This continued into my adult years. The only thing she added to the phrase was, "And don't bring that cellphone to this table!" I laughed but listened.

Sitting at her dining room table took me back to when my siblings and I gathered there as kids. Now adults, Granny's chairs were filled with a variety of visitors ranging from neighborhood kids to elderly friends. Many of the visits started in her living room and usually ended at her dining room table talking about her favorite subject: Jesus. To me, Granny's dining room table was sacred. If that table could talk, oh the stories it could tell.

Granny was a creature of habit, so I knew her routine like the back of my hand. After breakfast, she would clean the dishes, fix herself a hot drink, grab a Bible and spend time with the Lord. Usually, I went into another room, but on this day I decided to visit my uncle. Had I known what was in store, I may have stayed with Granny.

CHAPTER THIRTEEN

I DIDN'T MEAN TO KILL HIM

I threw on my shoes and made my way across the street. As I did, my grandfather was dropped off at my uncle's house. When I was a toddler, he had lost his vision and was declared legally blind. However, he did not let that stop him. He was incredibly skilled with his hands. Anytime I wanted to know where he was, most times I could find him in Granny's backyard fixing someone's lawnmower, snow blower and the like. Even without his sight, he could do amazing things.

He opened the car door. "What's up, Pop's?" I announced. (I dropped "Granddad" as I got older, and he did not seem to mind). With a hand on my shoulder and a walking stick in the other, we walked toward the house. Suddenly, he stopped. "Oh - that sounds like Virgil,"

I did not hear anything, just grunted in agreement, but the name did ring a bell.

I helped him inside the house and then walked back to Granny's home, rigorously racking my brain trying to recall the name. As

I got closer, I saw a man next door raking leaves in his front yard. When I finally got to Granny's driveway, an army of goose bumps met me there.

"Hey!" I blurted, pointing at him. "Is your name Virgil?" He looked as if he had seen a ghost. Before uttering a word, he dropped the rake and ran onto his porch, tripling our original twenty-foot distance. His reaction puzzled me. I had not approached him in an aggressive manner. Even when I pointed, it was not in a threatening or accusatory way, but his behavior confirmed my suspicions.

"Yeah, I'm Virgil!" he said with arrogance. I bounced my pointed finger slowly up and down in the air, "You're the guy who killed my dad!"

After serving sixteen years in prison, the parole board had granted him release, and he had moved back home. Never in my wildest dreams did I think I would ever come face to face with the man who killed my dad; the man whose one senseless act brought so much pain into the lives of so many.

Seeing him flipped the master switch to every feeling I had suppressed as a child, and my body literally shook from the surge. Every emotion in me fought for dominance. He was afraid and expected an angry response, but I had a surprise for him. He was going to die that day, yes… and I would be the one to kill him, not with a gun or a knife, like he used on Dad, but with kindness.

He lowered his head in what I thought to be shame, "I didn't mean to kill him," but no sooner than those words fell from his lips, he snapped his head up and said, "But you know he was cheating with my wife, right?"

When those words hit my ears, a flash of anger went through me like lightning, but as quick as it came it left in like manner. I remember thinking, *how can you tell the son of your victim something like this to justify your actions?* If he thought I was going to take his side and pat him on the back, then he had another thing comin'.

I shifted my weight to my right leg and leaned back on it while giving him a thorough appraisal. As I realized his face was one of the last Dad saw before leaving earth, I started to get angry. That was until I looked into his eyes. They were full of pain.

"Did he say anything before he died?" I asked. I always wondered what was on Dad's mind as his life ebbed away. I imagined one of his last thoughts was of my brother and me, but according to Virgil Dad said nothing.

My mind jumped to Granny. *What if she sees me talking to her son's killer?* I grew overwhelmed and no longer wanted to talk. I also did not want to give Virgil the satisfaction of seeing me cry.

As I was about to enter the house, he yelled from his porch, "If you ever wanna talk or hangout, let me know."

The excitement in his voice agitated me. "This guy thinks we're friends," I mumbled. I glared at him, amazed by his ridiculous request. If looks could kill, he would have dropped dead on sight. I stepped inside and slammed the door.

Emotionally wrung out and exhausted, with my back against the door, I slid to the floor. Overcome with grief, I dropped my head into my hands and wept. I then looked around and recalled every memory Dad and I shared in that room. My mind drifted to the things we missed: playing catch, him teaching me how to tie a necktie, and simply talking man to man. These are things I envision a father doing with his son, and we were robbed of them all.

I sat there reliving the horror of Dad's death when an interesting fact hit me like a Mack truck. "He never apologized," I seethed, clinching my fist. Virgil and I needed to get an understanding. Just as I stood to go next door, I heard Granny coming down the stairs. With haste, I dried my tears and put my glasses on to shield my puffy eyes.

All my life I have had the kind of relationship where I could tell Granny anything. One of her greatest qualities was her ability to keep a secret. Trust me, if Granny were a busybody, she would not have had the vast number of visitors in her home. She was a trustworthy woman, full of integrity and godly wisdom. That said, my apprehension to tell her was not because I did not trust her; it was because I did not know how she would react.

After wrestling with it for two days, I came clean. She responded by saying, "I'm not upset with you. We all have to get closure in our own way..." One thing she did make clear was Virgil was never married, so the lie he was selling, I was not buying.

We continued to talk, and she did her best to answer all my questions. Something I wanted to know was how she learned of Dad's passing.

"The day I got the news," she explained, "I was standing in my kitchen. I felt a tear come to one eye, and said, 'No, I can't cry. I have to be strong for everyone else.'"

Later in the conversation, I could almost hear the fibers in my heart tear when she admitted that, in all my foolishness, I had made her cry.

This was a monumental weekend, one I will never forget. There was a reason I met Dad's killer, but God would not reveal it until I hit rock bottom.

CHAPTER FOURTEEN

FREE CHOICE

The next few years were normal, at least to me. My life consisted of drinking booze, using drugs, and abusing the grace of God (see Jude 1:4). I slowed on drinking after nearly sideswiping a police officer while driving drunk, then eluding him somehow.

I was spending more time with worldly friends and was committing all sorts of sins. What made it even worse was the fact that I knew better. I was not sinning out of ignorance. I deliberately chose to wallow in the pigpen of sin, and the longer I stayed in there the harder my heart became toward the things of God. It was going to take something drastic to get my attention.

Now older, I was burned out on the club scene. Getting home in the wee hours of the morning, eardrums ringing from the loud music, had run its course. I did not want that life; I wanted something better. Unbeknownst to me, my famished soul yearned to be fed.

In John 10:10, Jesus said, *I have come that they may have life, and that they may have it more abundantly.* This abundant life is available to everyone; however, it is contingent upon us accepting Christ as our Lord and Savior, obeying His commands. He is not going to reward us for living a life of sin. It is only after we repent (turn from our sinful ways) and are free from the consequences of sin (salvation) that we obtain this abundant life.

God wants nothing but the best for us, and when we do not follow Him, He will do what is necessary to get us back on track. He can see beyond our human eyes and usually warns us before we make a mess of our lives. Still, it is within our power to choose.

Take a moment to reflect on a time you faced a major decision. Maybe it was financial, a relationship, job opportunity, etc. You had reservations but chose to silence the quiet voice in your head. In the beginning, your choice appeared to be wise but when things began to fall apart, you wished you had listened to the still, small voice.

More times than not, that voice is the Holy Spirit. He continually seeks to guide us toward Jesus. He will do whatever is needed to alert us when danger is around the corner. I have had many encounters like this, and one stands out.

It was a cold January night, the air was crisp, and the snowy, northeast Ohio skies were gray. I had just finished a long week at work and was looking forward to relaxing at home. However, the thought flew out the window when I learned one of my favorite bands would be performing at a local bar. I sent a text to a friend, and we made plans to attend.

To get in the mood, I turned on some music, grabbed a beer from the fridge and prepared to hit the town. My music was so loud that I barely heard my ringing phone.

The caller ID displayed the name of a friend I knew from church. He was a good, Christian man who I highly respected. It had been months since we spoke, and I wondered why he was calling. I debated about answering the phone, but my curiosity got the best of me. I answered, he said "hello" and then got right to the point. "Mike, God put you on my heart. I was wondering if you would be interested in joining me at church tonight." The seriousness of his voice pricked my conscience. I needed to end the call immediately.

"I'm sorry, but I have plans," I responded. "If something changes, I'll let you know."

"Okay, great!" he fired back. "I'll save you a seat!"

The nerves in my stomach churned after the call. I had grown all too familiar with the Holy Spirit's convicting power, and my quaking knees confirmed it.

I plopped down on the bed, shirt partially buttoned, and stared at a wall in deep thought. I will be the first to admit that my mental elevator did not always reach the top floor, but I was smart enough to know that this *random* call was not random at all. The Holy Spirit was clocked in and working overtime.

I released a sigh of frustration. *God, what are You up to?* Then my thoughts went in another direction. *What if God wants to spare me from something? What if I'm going to get into a car wreck, a bar fight, or some other tragedy?* The Spirit and my flesh were in a battle.

Finally, the Holy Spirit's voice grew to a loud crescendo. I had to make a choice. I could go to the bar, get drunk and not make it home, or I could go to church and get drunk on God's Spirit.

It did not take me long to decide; I chose the bar. I rationalized that if I went to church, I would be wondering who was at the bar and what songs the band was playing. My mind was already there so why not add my body to the equation.

Listen to me closely: the enemy is clever. When it comes to doing what is right, he will bring everything before you that you will miss. He will not tell you that the carrot of temporary pleasure he is dangling in front of you is leading you off a cliff. He will keep you focused on all the wrong things until that fatal step is made.

Forks in the road of life are inevitable. We all have them. It is when we make moves without God's help that we bring trouble into our lives.

Proverbs 3:5,6 tells us to *Trust in the Lord with all your heart, and lean not on your own understanding; In all your ways acknowledge Him, and He will direct your paths.* As you read earlier, for every problem God has a promise. The benefit of this promise is divine direction. If your dilemma is time sensitive, this rule still applies. Do not move until God makes it clear the way He wants you to go. He may even instruct you to wait. If we move without the Holy Spirit's guidance, it will no doubt take more time to untangle the mess we made.

That night I made a choice to stiff-arm God and embrace the devil and his people. I can say with 100% confidence that the choice I made to ignore God that night unequivocally changed the course of my life.

Every choice we make, good or bad, has a consequence. In that light, free choice really isn't free at all. At some point, we are going to pay.

CHAPTER FIFTEEN

TRIGGERED

I met my friend at the bar and had a few drinks while the band warmed up. I was in rare form. I bet my friend that I could get the phone number of any woman he pointed to. I was well on my way to winning the bet when the cutest girl I had seen all night walked in.

Gracefully she trotted by and sat at a table adjacent from ours. I tapped my friend and said, "Man, I want *her* number!" I got myself together and went to introduce myself, my nerves leading the way. "Hi, I'm Mike. It's nice to meet you. And you are..."

"Lacey," she said, extending her hand for a shake.

I smiled. "Lacey... that's a cute name."

Her cute name matched her elegant appearance. The light freckles on her cheeks made her unique, and her eyes... She had the most amazing eyes. One could easily get lost in them.

That night I called her, and our connection was immediate. Since my divorce, I had not given a female the time of day, as far as a relationship goes. It felt good talking to someone on a personal level, and Lacey made it easy.

One thing she did not mention was she had a boyfriend. I discovered this when I stopped by her place and saw him sitting on her couch. A normal person would have walked away, especially in the early stages, but I was not normal. I had a crippling fear of rejection, and a host of other issues. My eyes saw her boyfriend, but my brain saw my ex-wife rejecting me for my stepdad. This triggered something inside of me and it was not good.

Many of us have heard the phrase t*ime heals all wounds*. Well, in my case that could not be farther from the truth.

Think of your life as if it were a garden. If all you did was put seeds into the ground, covered them up, but never took time to water them, reaping a harvest of any kind should not be expected. The seed will only produce once proper care and adequate attention is given.

The same applies to you and me. Until we put in the work to deal with our issues, we will never improve regardless of how much time passes. The seeds, however, or issues planted in us, remain lodged in our heart. This is why I believe time does *not* heal all wounds. It is what is done in that time that heals them.

I had been divorced for over four years and made no effort to work on any of my problems. In my twisted thinking, I believed that if I could find a more compatible woman, everything would work itself out. Not once did I consider myself part of the problem.

Meeting Lacey while in this condition was unhealthy, not just for me but for her as well. Everything I had suppressed was being stirred up and was slowly rising to the surface.

We went back and forth about her boyfriend, and she finally cut the cord from him. Now that we were exclusive, we began living together. We had only met three weeks before and did not know much about each other.

Some of our commonalities were our godly grandmothers, failed marriages, and our inability to take the necessary steps to heal from past relationships. More importantly, we were both out of shape spiritually.

Our differences lay in our goals: she had them; I did not. She was spiritually ignorant; I was spiritually indifferent. I drank and used drugs; she rarely drank and was against drugs, even to the point of refusing medicine for headaches.

Being six years her senior, I had never considered being in a relationship with someone her age, but there was something special about her. She was mature and full of promise. Right away I could tell she was an academic genius, and I adored her compassion for others.

A couple months into our relationship, I shared with her how I lost Dad and how I had been struggling with it. About three days later, she surprised me with a photo album she had put together with pictures of him. Her thoughtfulness moved me to tears.

On the flip side, she could be equally abrasive with her words. To make it plain, she was a verbal assassin. I have yet to see anything like it. I voiced my aggravation about the way she spoke to me, and she admitted that it was a defense mechanism. If she felt someone was out to hurt her, she would try to hurt him or her first. This was not something she developed overnight. It was from things she never dealt with in her past.

These kinds of hurts, past or present, are not meant for us to manage alone. We do not have the power to heal, but we do have a God who can. When we try to fix them on our own, we move according to our emotions rather than the leadership of the Holy Spirit.

1 Peter 5:7 (NIV) says, *Cast all your anxiety on him because he cares for you.* When the Lord says "all," He means ALL! He did not tell us to handle the easy ones and give Him the rest. No. He told us to put *all* our concerns into His hands.

Four months into our relationship, Lacey learned she was pregnant. This would be her first child and my second.

I really enjoyed the pregnancy, maybe more than she did. I did not mind the late-night runs to Arby's to satisfy her mozzarella sticks and Dr. Pepper cravings. Even the mild mood swings were cute, within reason.

We found out we were having a girl and decided to name her Aubriana. The first time I heard her heartbeat, I was overcome with emotion. I could feel the corners of my eyes fill with tears as we watched her tiny hand wave at us on the ultrasound screen. Lacey and I talked like two giddy kids as the technician slipped out of the room. When she returned, in walked a doctor whose expressionless face brought us down to earth.

He squeezed a blob of gel on Lacey's stomach and turned his attention to the screen. "If you look here, all the stuff that looks like popcorn is actually intestines. It appears your daughter has what we call gastroschisis, a condition where the abdomen nearest the belly button does not close, leaving the intestines fully exposed. A surgeon will have to push them back manually and very carefully inside her body and stitch her stomach closed upon delivery."

This news was devastating but I did my best not to react. Lacey's demeanor mirrored the doctors. She was not one to show emotion, but I could tell the news affected her.

The doctor continued. "The average stay in the Neonatal Intensive Care Unit (NICU) is around three months. One of our concerns is the intestines absorbing too much amniotic fluid. For that reason, we will need to increase your checkups."

The word helpless does not do justice to how I felt. This was the first traumatic experience Lacey and I faced together, and without God in our lives it would be an even steeper hill to climb.

Since I was not used to affection, I felt uncomfortable showing it to others. It's not that I didn't want to, it's just that I didn't know how to.

I could see Lacey was hurting, so I stepped outside my normal and tried comforting her with a hug. She responded by pushing me away. This triggered my issues of rejection, and I coped the best way I knew how. I got high.

I was not on the best terms with God, so I asked Granny to pray for Aubriana. Members of Lacey's family were also praying, especially her dad.

Her dad was an amazing man. He had a captivating personality and was incredibly funny. We bonded over things like movies and old-school R&B music, but the Bible was our common ground. I did not live it, but I knew a lot about it.

Although Lacey had a tough exterior, she had a soft spot for her dad. I learned a lot about her by watching how they interacted.

On December 23, Aubriana was born. About ten minutes after her arrival, she was whisked to Akron Children's Hospital to undergo immediate surgery. By God's grace, and the prayers of family and friends, the surgery was a success.

The hospital put us in one of their suites that houses families with sick kids. By doing so, it allowed us to stay close while Aubriana recovered in the NICU just a few floors above. That was a tremendous blessing.

That year we spent Christmas in the NICU. It was different from any Christmas I had ever experienced, but it was one of the most memorable. Lacey and I really bonded.

After the surgery, the focus shifted to Aubriana's recovery. How well she recovered would determine her length of stay.

The first test was to see how her intestines digested milk. The milk was administered via a tube in her nose that went down to her stomach. One day it was good and the next day not so much. The one thing that never fluctuated was my level of stress.

The NICU was one big room and housed about ten babies. Our position gave us a view of everyone who entered. We were blessed to have the support of family and friends who came to visit. Just about every child got a visit, except for one baby.

This African American infant seemed to be in distress and cried constantly. I did not know why he was there, but he cried as if his life depended on it.

One day his crying became too much. Lacey had just given Aubriana a bath and put her to sleep when the little boy's crying woke her. Lacey, having to feed and recover, shook her head, and asked, "Where is his mother?"

A few days later, we got the answer to that question. The little child got his first visitor. It was a social worker who had come to speak to one of the nurses. The boy's mother was a drug addict and had abandoned her son. My heart bled for him. The love of a mother is so precious, and her addiction robbed her son of the love he rightfully deserved. He may have very well been crying for her.

This really hit home. I did not use drugs while Aubriana was in the hospital, and it gave me the ability to look at things from a sober perspective. I was seeing the forecast of my future if I did not heed this warning. That day, I told myself that I would never abandon my kids or allow drugs to take me away from them. Never say, "never."

Aubriana's recovery was really coming along. Her stomach was digesting the milk, and the swelling in her abdomen was subsiding quicker than expected. I'll never forget the words of a nurse after she examined Aubriana.

"I don't mean to sound rude," she explained, "but she is doing so well that we're expecting her to trip over the finish line."

When the hospital finally discharged her, we were told it was the second shortest stay for that condition in the history of Akron Children's Hospital. Aubriana's expected three months lasted two short weeks. Today, she is a walking miracle. To God be the glory.

James 5:15,16 says, *And the prayer of faith will save the sick, and the Lord will raise him up... The effective, fervent, prayer of a righteous man avails much.*

I learned much from this experience. Everything God allows us to go through is for our benefit. After all, how do we know the strength of a product if it is not tested? Of course, God knows, but He wants us to know. The purpose of every test is to increase our faith, deepen our dependency on God, draw us closer to Him, and bring glory to His name.

If you are in the middle of a test, don't just go through it, *GROW* through it. God is seeking to level you up in Him. When tests come, know this: God will not allow you to be tested without first giving you the strength to get through it. Furthermore, He will never leave you. He would not be a good Father if He abandoned us when we needed Him the most.

CHAPTER SIXTEEN

IS THIS HOW I AM GOING TO DIE

A couple years after Aubriana was born, the relationship between Lacey and I took a nosedive. I was in the clutches of addiction; she was often in the clutches of other men. My drug use was still in the dark, but slight changes in my behavior, like my exhaustive efforts to clean the house, began to make her suspicious.

One day I arrived home from work under the influence. Within minutes, she began to question my erratic behavior. She marched into the kitchen, grabbed a flashlight from underneath the sink and said, "Come over here, Michael Anthony. Let me see those eyes!"

I chuckled until she used my middle name, realizing she always meant business when doing so. I needed to come up with an excuse, apology, or both, and quick. Lying through my teeth, I claimed to have had a few drinks with the guys before coming home. The truth was alcohol played no part in the equation, but since she bought the excuse, it threw her off my trail, at least for the time being.

In order to bring life to the lie, I had to drink at home but did so when she was there. With the facade in place, I would go into the bathroom under the guise of showering. I was really going in there to do a couple of lines. The running water was only there to mask the sound of snorting cocaine.

Now that I was back to drinking on a regular basis, it was ironic that the fake addiction I had created to mask the real addiction, actually became an addiction. I now craved alcohol as much as I craved cocaine. Way to go, Mike!

There was a lot of insanity going on in my brain. For me to come up with a new addiction to hide my real addiction from Lacey, knowing that alcohol would be more socially acceptable than cocaine, was insane.

It got to the point that, if I did not have a beer after work, it would ruin the rest of my night, and by proxy Lacey's night. On more than one occasion, she would ask, "Do you have to drink every day?" The simple answer was *yes*, but I interpreted her inquiry as nagging. The typical response to this would be to get defensive and shut down, making it seem like it was her fault. Discussing my alcohol addiction, which was also a cocaine addiction, led to many arguments.

Addicted minds think differently. Somehow, in my twisted thought process, at least in reference to my addiction, drinking alcohol was a twofold blessing. It gave me a shield to hide my drug use behind, and it helped dull the pain with what Lacey and I were going through. It was not her fault I was an addict, yet I blamed her internally for driving my substance abuse. Of course, this was not true because I was using before we met.

I was not the only one with an addiction, though. It seemed to me that Lacey's addiction was one of attention. She craved it from men. This grew into bigger problems when she had been unfaithful to me with several of these men. When you couple this with my addiction, our relationship became a lit stick of dynamite ready to blow.

During these dark days with Lacey, I reflected on the tragic death of my past marriage. Even though it was not my fault, I still shouldered the blame for my ex-wife having an affair with my stepdad. I concluded there was just something about me that made me unlovable.

The thought of being without Lacey petrified me; I had become dependent on her. I was afraid if I did not have her in my life, I would never find anyone who was willing to tolerate and love me. From a logical standpoint, it did not make sense that I would feel the need to have her in my life, because of how she treated me. Was it only infatuation? Leaving, however, was not an option. I only needed a mental getaway.

Turning to my base instincts, I asked around and found a guy who claimed to have just what I needed: heroin. We met at a gas station, and he handed me a small baggie. I simultaneously handed him some cash. According to him, the product he sold me was comparable to the high-octane gas that filled his 1994 GT Mustang. Perhaps there was a hidden meaning behind us meeting at a gas station, and him likening his illicit product to high-octane gasoline. Whatever the case may have been, I did not have time to think about that. I had to get high.

Having a rather severe fear of needles at the time, I opted out of shooting the drug, choosing instead to snort it. By now, the effects of cocaine were all too predictable and less reliable. I felt I was achieving a penultimate high, which was satisfactory, but I needed more. I need the ultimate high. I needed a high that would not just numb my body but my mind and soul as well. That agent, I heard from fellow addicts over the years, should be heroin.

There I was ready to try the dangerous drug for the first time, and because I was so green, the dealer offered to measure out my first dose.

You ask, 'how insane was it for me to let a guy who I just met measure out the dangerous narcotic that was going into my body?' Very!

My first time with heroin was not going to take place in a parking lot. I wanted privacy, so I returned home; and, finding the house empty, I headed to the bedroom. I ingested a small amount, half of his measured dose because it did not feel right to trust what he did. It ended up delivering such a devastating blow to my system that I plummeted to the floor, writhing in pain while beginning to sweat profusely. In all my drunken nights and frequent blackouts, I had never felt the urge to vomit as I did then. How I mustered the strength to crawl into the bathroom, only God knows.

My stomach churned in spasmodic pain as I hovered on the toilet. Seeing my reflection in the water was rather symbolic; this was where my life was headed. I clung to the rim of the bowl for what seemed like an eternity but was about twenty-five minutes until the nausea subsided. I had dodged a bullet.

Knowing I could have died had I taken the full dosage from my friendly neighborhood dealer made me angry, angry enough to inflict permanent damage to his body.

Still feeling horrible, I retrieved the baggie of heroin from my pocket, dumped its contents into the toilet water, and watched it swirl out of sight, along with my reflection. That night I made a promise never to touch heroin again. This is a promise I would keep. The mental escape I was seeking would come from some other chemical, and I would search until I found it.

One year after this, I received word that the Drug Enforcement Agency (DEA) had the same heroin dealer from whom I had copped under surveillance. When one of his buyers overdosed and died from his product, the DEA did what I wanted to do, kick down his door and take him captive. He was later sentenced to fourteen years in prison.

For some sick reason I took pleasure in the news, not in the demise of the victim, but in the fact that I had cheated death. The Grim Reaper had come for me, and I was perspicacious enough to elude him. A sick grin plastered my face as I beat my chest in pride. I was so stuck on myself that I could not see God stepping in on my behalf. I thought it was my own doing.

During all of this, I was blindsided by a notice I received in the mail. It was a legal document letting me know that my ex-wife requested to move to Florida, taking our daughter with her. The first time I read it, I was in a state of shock. Once I read it again, I became angry. Part of the anger stemmed from knowing she was a more suitable parent than I was. I did not approve of some of her actions, but I believed she was a good mother.

The news incited panic. Just about all my extra money went to feed my addiction. I had no savings for an attorney.

What I heard about court appointed counsel: they were nothing but a joke. I felt hopeless and did not believe I had a chance. It felt like, no matter where I turned, life consistently disrespected me. Why had God spared me from the heroin overdose? Was it to continue punishing me? Whatever sick game He was playing, I wanted nothing of it.

My stress was at an all-time high. By now, you do not need me to tell you how I coped. The pattern was predictable. Get into trouble? Drugs and booze. Feel anxious? Drugs and booze. Stressed with Lacey? Drugs and booze. Anything happening that displeases me? Drugs and booze. Cocaine was the ersatz safety blanket I carried everywhere.

I never used drugs to make my problems go away. It was the *I don't care* mind frame I was after. Once the high diminished, every problem I had was there to greet me, and bigger.

By the time I readied myself to respond to the courts notice, it was too late. My ex-wife's request was granted by default. The stress that could have been temporary had become a deep permanent sadness.

I left the courthouse in a daze. It seemed as if the walk to my car was in slow motion. *How could I have been so stupid? All I had to do was show up and at least the court would have acknowledged my presence and given me a chance to respond.* Dejected and disgusted with myself, I began the trip home, refusing to look in the rearview mirror.

The sun was shining, but my disposition was dark and moody. As I drove away, I gave in and looked in the mirror which brought light to reality. The Municipal Courthouse slowly shrank away just like the time with my daughter. Stupid mirror! I would conjure up every excuse I could that did not point to me. The blame wheel I had spun so many times before finally landed on God and drugs, not on me. They were the cause of all of this: God, for allowing years of misfortune in my life; and drugs for how they had stolen from me.

The thought of not seeing my daughter tortured me to no end. One of the last moments we shared played repeatedly in my mind. We were sitting on the floor, shoulder to shoulder, while playing with her baby dolls. Out of nowhere, she paused, then looked at me, and said in her cute but tiny voice, "Dad, will you be my best friend?" I was so taken aback by her sincerity that I could not answer right away. I tried to respond but the words got trapped behind a lump in my throat. I coughed to jar them loose.

"Of course!" I boldly declared. "Will *you* by *my* best friend?"

"Of course!" she rejoiced.

I wept bitterly over this memory. Every ounce of guilt and shame I felt had been earned. I was the one person who should have been there for her, and I failed. Now she was moving to a new state with no family or friends, and without me, her best friend. Some dad I was, huh?

Unfortunately, I added my daughter to the growing list of casualties due to my selfishness. Before this, I did not think I had a problem with drugs or alcohol because I was still going to work, paying my bills, and not breaking any laws. The way I handled the situation with my first daughter helped me see that I did have a problem.

Recognizing a problem and doing something about it are two very different things. Right then, I decided not to duplicate the same parenting mistakes with Aubriana as I made with my first daughter but, unbeknownst to me, the hand had already begun to write on the wall.

Behind my fake, plastic smile was a damaged individual. Fights between Lacey and me were escalating, with some of them of a physical nature on both sides. I hated the way she belittled me when she got angry or when things did not go her way. Instead of retaliating on those passive aggressive confrontations, I stuffed them on whatever space I had left on my mental shelf. Due to this, I began to resent her.

Back when Lacey was pregnant with Aubriana, even before we found out the gender, we both hoped for a boy. After learning we were having a girl, she looked me in the face and said with a scowl, "I knew you weren't man enough to give me a boy!"

I literally rolled my shoulders to shake it off but deep down her words got next to me. The longer I held on to them, and other rude remarks she had made, the more I despised her.

Ephesians 4:26 says, *Be angry, and do not sin. Do not let the sun go down on your wrath*. This is a powerful warning. When we allow debris in our mind to settle in our soul, the potential for terrible things to happen grows exponentially.

Most men are not willing to admit they are or have been in verbally abusive relationships. Perhaps this is because it does not sound manly, or people would not believe it, but I had to come to grips with the fact of what type of relationship I was in, Toxic.

Lacey's degrading words took what little was left of my self-esteem, ground it into a fine powder, and she blew it into the wind. The best thing for me to do was walk away, but instead I used Aubriana as an excuse to stay. Already one daughter had been lost through neglect. I was not taking a chance of losing another. I loved my family. When things were great, family was great. When things were bad, family was awful.

Although I did not intend to leave for good, I did try to wiggle away from time to time. I would usually save my long nights of partying until Lacey went to visit family, which was out of town. Normally, her visits would last the entire weekend. When I did not tag along, it allowed me time to use drugs with peace of mind. (As I put together "use drugs" and "peace of mind," I realize how insane it sounds, but that's how it was back then.)

One weekend, Lacey and Aubriana went out of town, leaving me to my own devices. Most times, the plan would be to stay home and drink, but the newly renovated bar down the street was calling my name. With time and opportunity in my favor, I threw on a pair of jeans and walked to the bar. As I approached the parking lot, it was full of Harley Davidson motorcycles. This was not my type of crowd, but I was there to drink, not socialize. I already felt out of place, if you know what I mean, and the evil feeling that washed over me as I entered did not help.

Thinking it was only in my mind, I took to the nearest bar stool, ordered a beer, and tried to acclimate to the environment. After I knocked a couple back, the alcohol fueled a euphoric feeling that freed me to party.

Back in the 1960s, companies started making dolls with strings attached to their back and a plastic loop to pull on to make the doll come alive and talk. This is what booze did to me. It pulled my string, and all I could think about was getting high. This was where I was at, looking for coke. The timing could not have been better. If I had had one more drink, I am sure I would have blacked out. That was not the place for that to happen.

I looked for a bartender so I could close my tab, go get my car, and find some coke. As I spun the stool around, a man in my peripheral vision took my attention. For whatever reason, I sensed a strong connection to him. My gaze was interrupted by the tapping on the table from the bartender. I gave her my card and while waiting for her to return, the mystery man approached. "Hey. Cool Mohawk!" (Yes, I had a Mohawk.) I ignored the compliment.

"Do you have any weed?" I questioned. (If you recall, I don't like weed. This was only to feel him out).

"No!" he answered, "But I have coke!"

BINGO! For the rest of the night, we got high off his supply. I learned the reason he had so much was because he was a drug dealer. If that was not bad enough, he lived one block from me. Why weren't we best friends already? From that moment forward, I identified with that evil feeling.

On many of the nights I would party, I ran out of drugs. I would call my dealer and we would agree to meet at a strip club where I made the score. With pockets full of cocaine that night, I headed to my car when that same evil feeling came over me. Something told me to go into the bar across the street. Because I was prone to give into this feeling again, it compelled me to go.

I obeyed.

As I stood in the doorway to survey the room, a short, petite woman on the dance floor stood out. I stopped. It was only a matter of seconds before our eyes locked, and I made a beeline for her. Though I was moving quickly, there was still time for me to size her up. (*She looks like she parties... Cocaine is the answer*). What would my opening line be? My first words to this gorgeous woman were, "Do you want to do some coke?"

She stopped dancing and looked at me. "You're like the third person to ask me that tonight," she said.

Ten minutes later, we were outside getting high. I was delighted in the fact that out of the three, she chose me. My ego ran wild, but that would not last. It never does when built on a pile of cocaine, because there is no substance to it. It is only *a* substance.

Many years have passed, and at times I think about that young woman. I pray she has a relationship with Jesus and is not trapped under the armpit of addiction due to my stupidity.

I did not realize it then, but I was giving myself more and more to the devil with every senseless decision. I was also beginning to influence those around me. If you were not covered by the blood of Jesus, the odds of me working you over were in my favor. I was fully aware of this.

Lacey called to let me know that her visit had ended early, and she would be home soon. I stopped what I was doing and rushed home to straighten up. She already had her fill of my drinking, so the empty beer bottles in the trash would be a dead giveaway that I had too much fun while she was away.

With the house back in order, I focused on the rest of the night. I still had more partying to do, so I began thinking of ways to shake loose without starting a nuclear war. Oh, you can believe there would be consequences, but if I maneuvered right, they would be minimum. That is the power of addiction.

Lacey was almost in town when I called her. I suggested we meet for dinner and was glad when she agreed. It would be easier to slip away since I would already be out.

When Lacey and Aubriana arrived, their smiling faces gave me second thoughts about going out. Even though we were only apart for a day and a half, I did miss them. Those thoughts were aborted, however, when Lacey began to interrogate me about how I spent my time away from her.

I was glad Lacey had picked the restaurant that she did. I would need something heavy in my system to hold the beer down since the cocaine would suppress my appetite later.

Aubriana munched on her chicken fingers, I baptized my ribs in BBQ sauce, and Lacey cut into her (very) expensive steak. I grew antsy thinking about the night ahead and grabbed my phone to check the time when suddenly, for no apparent reason, it shut off. I attempted to resuscitate it to no avail. This was *not* part of the plan.

I concentrated solely on fixing the phone until I looked across the table and saw Lacey's stare (which should be banned in all fifty states.) "Are you serious right now?" she said. Completely baffled, I put the phone away and chalked it up as a loss; however, my frown turned upside down when I realized the phone problem might work in my favor. I would not have to ignore Lacey's calls because they would not come through. And since she saw it with her own eyes, she would know I was telling the truth. This was perfect.

With our plates clean and bellies full, I paid the bill and waddled to the car with the girls. Lacey spoke of what she wanted to do once we were home, but little did she know that I would not be there for a few more hours.

I fastened Aubriana into her car seat and cleaned the chocolate milk mustache from her face before planting an exaggerated kiss on her cheek. I made sure it was wet enough to wipe it off. You know, like the ones we used to get as children.

I approached Lacey, wondering what to do next. The longer I stalled, the more obvious it became that I was up to no good, but I couldn't just leave. My exit needed timed exactly right. When Aubriana whined about needing to go potty, I attempted a jump through my window of opportunity, only to get stuck.

With a kiss and an attempt to close her door, Lacey extended her arm to stop me. "I know you're up to something, Michael Anthony. Where are you trying to run off to?" I could tell from the way she looked at me when I kissed her that she knew I was saying goodbye, which is why I rushed to close her door.

Knowing she was studying me like a final exam, I spat out the first thing that came to mind and paused for a positive reaction. It never came. Whether or not I went home was immaterial. I was now in the doghouse for even wanting to go out.

I administered another kiss, this time to her forehead, and promised to see them later. She grabbed the door, slammed it shut, nearly catching me in it. Although she was angry, I was glad she pulled away first. It would minimize the risk of being followed.

With no phone, I had no choice but to show up to the dealer unannounced. This is not ideal. Most drug users, as dealers often are, suffer from acute bouts of paranoia. The last thing you want to do is startle them. Many times, they are armed.

I knocked until I saw a pair of red eyes peer from behind a curtain. At last, the door swung open. I entered and was welcomed with a beer. A room full of drug users toasted to signify the festivities had officially begun.

What more could an addict want? There was a pile of cocaine and cheap booze in the fridge. What could go wrong? Plenty! Most often when I used cocaine for an extended amount of time, my hands would tingle, and my chest would tighten. I needed these symptoms for multiple reasons. If I did not get them, I would have known the product was overly cut (cut meaning other foreign substances like powdered sugar, crushed drywall, baby formula and the like which adds volume to the product but lessens its potency), and I had been duped. But the main reason? It was my cue to slow down between lines because I tended to get overzealous.

In addition to the booze and coke, someone set out a couple joints. I stuck to my usual and did not consider smoking, but the higher I became, the better it looked. When the joint came around, I jumped in the rotation and took two big puffs. My tolerance for marijuana did not exist. I was so discombobulated that I missed the signal my body was giving me to stop snorting coke.

Suddenly, it felt like an anvil had landed on my chest, and I was stuck under it. I went outside, my friends in tow, hoping fresh air would do the trick. It did not.

Everything grew dark, darker than the 3 a.m. that blanketed us. I became lightheaded and sensed myself falling to the ground, when a voice in my head said, "Michael, you've got to stay up!", and somehow, I did.

I stumbled up the steps and made my way into the kitchen. Turning on the cold-water full blast, I started lapping it like the dog that I had become. Driving me was the thought of dying by an overdose and going to a real, burning hell. I drank as much water as I could, but it did not seem like enough. Leaning on the counter to catch my breath, I felt the phone in my pocket. I pulled it out with the intent to dial 911, but it refused to turn on.

I went back outside and asked my so-called friends for their phone but was denied. Just then, I saw headlights approaching. Flailing my arms like a mad man, I stood in the road and flagged down the driver. I begged him for a ride to a hospital, and he cursed me out and sped off. *Is this how I am going to die?*

Finally, the female friend saw my desperation and gave me her phone. I dialed 911. As best I could, I told the dispatcher what drugs I had taken and what symptoms I was having. With urgency she replied, "Sir, where are you?" I was quiet. Again, "Sir, where are you? We need to know where to send help," she pleaded.

For reasons unclear to me at the time, I could not remember where I was for the life of me. Running would only intensify the pain in my chest so I walked swiftly to the corner. On a pole was a street name. I tried reading it to the dispatcher but couldn't. My cognitive skills were fading.

Out of frustration I ended that call and walked back to the house. I had just about given up until I saw a Bible lying on the backseat of my car. *That's it! That's what I need: supernatural help!"* I nearly yanked the door handle off as I dove on top of it, desperately hugging it to my bosom.

With the Bible clutched to my chest, I fell on my knees, raised my hand and head toward heaven, and begged God for mercy. I stared into the sky and was at once struck by all the bright stars. The way they twinkled made me feel as if the God who created them was listening.

With hope renewed, I stood to my feet with more peace than I had before I prayed. It did not happen immediately, but I felt strength returning to my body. When I spun around, my two friends were sitting with their eyes closed, appearing to have been praying with me. Once they saw I was okay, one of them ran into the house and brought out some beers. I told them I was done. All I could think about was seeing Lacey and Aubriana. I needed to get home.

It was close to 4:30 in the morning when I arrived home. I knew I would have to pay for my sins with Lacey but did not have it in me to do it that morning. She would be livid and rightfully so, but I needed to sleep so my body and mind could recoup.

I unlocked the door, and it opened, partially. She had fastened the chain on the door. *Great, so much for me sneaking in. Now I have to wake her.* With no phone, I tossed a pebble at the window. The creaking of the stairs let me know she was on her way. She opened the door without incident. Using her quiet, but stern voice so as not to awaken Aubriana, she immediately demanded answers.

"Michael, it's almost five in the morning. Where were you? I've been calling you all night, and you kept sending me to your voicemail." (I almost interjected and reminded her of my broken phone but there was no point.) "Where were you? And don't lie to me! I want the truth!"

Completely drained, I told her everything (I felt like Samson when he told Delilah the secret to his superhuman strength. See Judges 14-17). I struggled to get the words out between sobs, as I shared how God had saved me. If she needed ammo to go berserk, I loaded the gun and put it into her hands, but she remained calm. Deep down, I believe she knew I was abusing drugs but wanted to hear it from me. It got to the point that I could no longer speak, just cry. I could have died, and God saved me.

I regained my composure, went into Aubriana's room, and found her fast asleep. She looked peaceful, without a care in the world. With a new appreciation for life, I watched as her chest swelled up and down and thanked God for giving me more time with her. I gently kissed her before joining Lacey in bed.

I tried to fall asleep, but my mind was still wired for sound. I lay there restless when Lacey wrapped her arm around me and put her hand on my rapidly beating chest. I flinched with pain and was about to remove her hand when she tightened her grip as to say, Honey, it's okay, I've got you. You're safe now.

Finally, I closed my eyes and fell asleep. Yes, with pain in my heart, but praise on my lips.

CHAPTER SEVENTEEN

SIN IS CROUCHING AT YOUR DOOR

The next day I was awakened by Aubriana jumping on the bed, ordering me to get up. If she only knew what I had gone through a few hours earlier. Nevertheless, I promptly got up, opened the curtains, and took in the Sunday morning sunrise. I was just thankful to see another day and took in God's glory and splendor. The warmth, the rays bouncing off leaves on the tree outside the window. The clouds, clouds I had never taken time to look at before now had value. This simple, yet beautiful, moment seemed to energize my entire being. I was alive again.

Lacey lay in bed covering her ears with a pillow, begging Aubriana to quiet down so she could sleep, which was not going to happen. Once Aubriana was up, she was up.

I took her into the kitchen and made breakfast. Moments later, Lacey entered, eyes barely open, practically sleepwalking. I wooed her with her favorite: biscuits, scrambled eggs with sausage gravy topped with shredded cheddar cheese. I mean, would you be able to sleep with all that flavorful goodness floating in the air? She loved my recipe, and I could use the brownie points after my screw-up the night before.

Lacey was quieter than normal. I did not know if it was because of my late-night escapade or from lack of sleep, but I did my best to keep the conversation moving.

In the midst of a dead moment came a thought that had not entered my brain in a long time. I was thinking about going to church, and the more it marinated with me, the more I thought about being around other believers and worshipping God.

Discerning the origin of this thought was simple. When Satan wanted me to do something, it felt like he shoved me in the back and walked behind me with a gun. Although I had a choice, it seemed as if he was making sure I fulfilled whatever sinful act he laid out. That's the evil of addiction.

The Holy Spirit was entirely different. His nudges were soft, gentle, free of condemnation, and always about the right thing. I imagined Him putting His arms around my shoulders as if He were my father, and He was. My Father.

Last night when I dropped to my knees and stretched my hands toward heaven, desperate for help, God showed me compassion and reached down from His throne to save me. To the human eye nothing changed. The heavens did not split, the earth did not quake, and I may have even looked the same, but God rebuilt me on the inside and installed all new parts.

The first thing to change were my desires. The Holy Spirit knocked the glitter off the old sinful deeds I once enjoyed, making them look downright disgusting. I wanted to live a life that pleased God, not myself. 2 Corinthians 5:17 says, *Therefore, if anyone is in Christ, he is a new creation: old things have passed away; behold, all things have become new.* The blood of Jesus had made me new.

I finished breakfast, hopped in the shower, and, for the first time in a long time, without drugs. As the water ran over my body, I imagined the blood of Jesus washing away every sin I had ever committed. If you don't understand Christianity, this blood thing can give you pause, but it is this way; before I accepted Christ, I felt worthless, but the Holy Spirit pointed me to the cross where Jesus shed His blood and proved I was worth His sacrifice. It was finished.

I told Lacey about me wanting to go to church, but she did not say much. Perhaps she did not believe me, and I could not blame her. Would you? I got dressed, kissed them goodbye, then walked to my car with a little more pep in my step. I did not know what church I was going to, but I knew I was going to church.

As I drove along, a familiar noise sounded from beneath the seat. I turned the radio off to make sure I was not hearing things.

"You have got to be kidding!" I said aloud. Reaching under my seat, I picked up my cellphone which was on… beeping with notifications. All I could do was laugh. Not a *funny* laugh, but one of complete bewilderment and amazement. This only confirmed what I knew to be true; Satan tried to kill me, and God intervened.

A righteous anger came over me, and I shouted at the top of my lungs, "SATAN, YOU SHOULD HAVE KILLED ME WHEN YOU HAD A CHANCE!", and I meant every word. With my face contorted in anger against the devil, I glanced at a car next to me. The driver was staring as if I had five heads. It was an awkward encounter, to say the least, and all I could think to do was smile and give a quick wave, but, before I dropped my hand, he floored his car through the green light.

With the car gone, a church came into view that I had never noticed before. The sign was too seminal to ignore. I would be attending a service there. Though the church building was small, it proved to be mighty in power.

Inside, the singers sang their hearts out, and the pastor preached the roof off. Every word he spoke brought more of the Holy Spirit's conviction on me. There were things in my life that were out of alignment with Scripture. If I was to follow Christ, I needed to make some changes. Many changes. I knew the truths of Scripture. I left the service knowing what I had to do and would need God's help to do it.

1 Thessalonians 5:22 (KJV) tells us to abstain from all appearances of evil. Living together before marriage does not coincide with this verse. My days of shacking up needed to end.

The Holy Spirit also convicted me of my sexual activity. 1 Corinthians 6:9 (KJV) explains how those who commit fornication (sex outside of marriage) will not get into the kingdom of God.

Society encourages couples to live together and to have sex before marriage. After all, how do you know if you want the car if you don't test drive it, right? That used to be a saying years ago, and now most of society delays or is against marriage.

Today's youth, especially, are being influenced by sex more than any generation to have walked the earth. From TV shows, movies, social media, and other forms of entertainment, they are being influenced, and in today's world, fornication is as common as a handshake.

To the young who are reading this, guard your innocence. Wait until you are married to have sex. If you have already crossed that line, now that you know what Scripture says about it, with

God's help, you can do things right from this moment forward. If the person you are with truly loves you, they will honor your belief in God's Word and respect your morals.

When you follow Christ, He will guide you to the mate He has chosen for you. After all, He knows you better than you know yourself and has your needs in mind when He selects your mate. Matthew 6:33 says, *But seek first the kingdom of God, and his righteousness, and all these things shall be added to you.* Only when God is in the number one spot in our lives will things begin to fall into place, and not a second sooner.

Let's be real. It would all be very difficult, every aspect of it. I was more comfortable committing the act than I was not committing it if that makes sense, but. Luke 1:37 says, *With God nothing will be impossible.* (Luke 1:37.)

I did not know how to break the news about me moving out to Lacey, so I just ripped the Band-Aid off as fast as I could. We spent the rest of the day together, but the dark cloud that loomed over us was evident. As night drew nearer, I would have to say goodbye.

The hardest part was not the packing of my belongings like I thought it would be. It was walking out on Aubriana, at least that's what my brain told me I was doing. She could not understand what was taking place. Why does doing the right thing sometimes feel so wrong? I tell you, going against the grain of our flesh to obey the Holy Spirit can be brutal.

Several days after I moved, I realized my craving for drugs and alcohol had vanished. God clearly did for me what I could not do for myself. Any addict out there knows how hard this is to believe, but it happened.

Lacey became so inspired by what God was doing in me that she began attending church as well. Aubriana had a blast in the kids' church and always had a new song to teach us.

Like me, she was born with a love for music. When Lacey was pregnant with her, she would always kick when her college professor played music from symphony great, Sebastian Bach.

She was a little tyke when we enrolled her into a private Christian school. Her talent for singing got her picked to perform a duet at a school function. *Tell Me the Story of Jesus*, was the song she and a friend sang, and did so in front of a crowd of hundreds. It was quite a task for a four-year-old, but she did an amazing job. I was so proud of her.

In addition to her regular education, she was learning a lot about God in school and at church. One evening, I took her to a park to feed the ducks. We stood hand in hand on the riverbank and tossed food with our other hand. Amid the ducks flew in a Canadian goose. Aubriana gasped as the goose hopped toward us on the only leg it had.

"Dad, what happened to its leg?" she asked with concern.

"I'm not sure. It probably lost it in a fight or something," I replied, focused more on the kayakers paddling downstream.

Suddenly, her body jerked pulling me in her direction. She pointed at the disabled goose and shouted, "JESUS, HEAL THIS GOOSES LEG!" A few moments later, she bent down, looked under its belly, and then looked at me with the cutest confused face I had ever seen.

"Dad, why didn't his leg grow back?" Her genuineness melted my heart, and her faith mesmerized me. Not only did she believe God to restore the missing leg, but she also expected it to happen immediately.

The pure, expectant faith Aubriana displayed is the faith we followers of Christ are to have. In Luke 18:16,17 (NIV), Jesus said, *Let the little children come to me, and do not hinder them, for the kingdom of heaven belongs to such as these. Truly I tell you, anyone who will not receive the kingdom of God like a little child will not enter it.*

If we humble ourselves and believe like a child, there is no telling what God will do in our lives. I would not be surprised to learn on that Great Day that God did restore the goose's leg. Because of the way Aubriana prayed, I too want that duck, duck, goose kind of faith.

Sadly, as days turned to months, my stance of abstaining from sex became harder and harder. Looking back, I should have seen this coming. I was neglecting my time in the Word and was not praying consistently like I was when God saved me. Because of this, my spiritual strength waned. Like Samson, I did not know my strength was gone until it was too late.

The apostle Paul said it perfectly: *You were running a good race. Who cut in on you to keep you from obeying the truth?* (Galatians 5:7 NIV). I started out well, but when I fell, instead of getting up, I gave up.

If things in your spiritual walk seem out of order, check your daily routine. It is hard to tell how many of life's problems come from neglecting daily prayer and Bible reading. If you are not where you should be, don't fret. You can start improving right now. *Now is the day of salvation* (2 Corinthians 6:2.) Every day is the right day.

Instead of repenting and asking God to forgive me, I threw up my hands and continued to disobey. I was going to church, but not for the right reasons. I lost the zeal I once had after God saved me and only went to collect the $250 I was paid to perform with the band each Sunday.

In the music world, most prospects come through word of mouth, and your reputation is everything. If you want to remain in good standing, be on time, play your position, and never quit without giving notice.

I accepted a gig at another church and for no real reason and without giving notice, I quit. The entire experience lasted two and a half weeks. To this day, it is the only musical endeavor I walked away from in this manner, but as you will find out later, the fingerprints of God were all over this.

With my relationship with God strained, I went back to what I was used to doing, pleasing my flesh. I stayed away from cocaine due to my overdose, but I did resume drinking. The priorities in my life had changed but I had definitely slid backward. I just did not make time for God anymore.

With Him in my rearview mirror, life seemed easier. I did not feel the constant tug of war between good and evil, which was a relief. I was making good money; Aubriana was healthy and growing like a weed, and, after graduating from college, Lacey had found a good job.

A few months into the new job, she came home talking about a male coworker. The story was of no significance but the way her face lit up was. At the time, I did not make anything of it, but I did file it away for future reference.

Approximately one year into the job, she took a temporary leave to go back to school. After passing an exam, she enrolled into law school and was accepted. We were both ecstatic about the news. Part of me was also glad she would be away from the male coworker.

Several weeks later, we learned she was pregnant for a second time. During one of the prenatal checkups, the doctor noticed some complications. He removed his glasses, and then rubbed his eyes in confusion. "And this is the same dad," he questioned. To me, the way Lacey answered "yes" was unsettling.

Soon after, Lacey's blood pressure skyrocketed to stroke levels. I stopped what I was doing and rushed her and Aubriana to the hospital.

While waiting for a nurse in the hospital room, Aubriana looked at me and began to giggle. "Look, Dad," said while wrapping her entire hand around my two fingers and leading me to a mirror. I was overcome with laughter. I then turned to Lacey, where she too began laughing. No wonder, I had pink blush and purple lipstick all over my face from the makeover Aubriana had been giving me before this emergency. Thanks a lot, Aubrey.

Less than ten hours later, Olivia was born. She was a few weeks early but healthy, nonetheless. The surgeon briefly held her in the air, giving us a peek, before passing her to a nurse. I followed the nurse into another room where she placed Olivia under a heat lamp and gave her a shot of caffeine to help keep her alert. If she ever develops a strong taste for coffee, I'll know why.

Due to her premature birth, Olivia was placed in the NICU. Akron Children's Hospital had rebuilt a wing of their hospital and moved the NICU into it. Instead of newborns clumped together in a large room, they had individual suites for each family.

Our suite was spectacular. Located on the top floor, it gave us a bird's eye view of the city. Everything we needed, they provided: food, shower, TV, room service, bed, and the most amazing staff. There was no need to leave the room unless we chose to. Akron Children's Hospital is truly a state-of-the-art facility. Thank you.

Olivia spent her eight days there inside an incubator. If I could, I would have jumped in with her. She looked so peaceful. Her big, bold, beautiful brown eyes drew me in like a magnet, and the way Aubriana interacted with her new sister through the Plexiglas was precious. The thing that tugged on my heartstrings the most was when she would open the hand slot and sing to her. It took everything in me not to cry.

The best part of any of the days was our skin-to-skin time. The skin-to-skin method promotes bonding between the parent and newborn. Olivia would be stripped to her diaper, I would sit in a recliner, and a nurse would place her on my bare chest, usually through the neck of my T-shirt. Within minutes, she was sound asleep. Every parent knows a child does not usually fall asleep unless he or she is at peace and has a feeling of security. This was always the pinnacle of my day.

The weight of raising a newborn and attending law school became too much. After five months, Lacey decided to put that part of her life on hold. I never doubted her capabilities to complete it because, at least academically, she had the Midas touch.

She returned to the same job and unfortunately the communication with the male coworker resumed. It began with constant texting while she was home, which led to many intense arguments between us. "We're just friends!" was her usual line of defense, but things were not adding up.

One evening, Lacey and I were enjoying a rare drama free night at home. I had been drinking which removed my filters. Alcohol was my truth serum. I began to verbalize some of my innermost thoughts, wondering if we could somehow iron out the problems in our relationship. (I could never grasp that it takes two to make a relationship work).

By this time, we had been engaged twice, each of them ending at her behest. Perhaps it was the beers talking, but I wanted to make our family official for our kids as much as for myself. Somehow, with this beer brain, I felt getting married would make her commit to me.

At the time, Olivia was almost a year old. I was thirty-four years old and tired of playing house. It was time to make the relationship legal and turn our house into a home.

Lacey never answered. Instead, she abruptly changed the subject. Though I felt dejected, I did not broach the topic again.

While at work the next day, she sent me a text which read, "We need to talk!" I never had a problem with these four words, but in this format, I hated them.

The workday ended, and I could not get home fast enough. Lacey was waiting in the kitchen when I got there. Not knowing what to expect, I leaned against a wall and braced for impact. She made no eye contact. This was not going to be good.

With no numbing agent to dull the pain, she delivered the news in its rawest form.

"I know you've been talking about being a family and wanting to get married, but there's something you should know." Time stood still, then she made the confession. "I've been sleeping with someone else."

My stomach dropped to my ankles and my bowels almost gave way. How did I not collapse? Thank God for that wall. "How long?" I probed, moving my trembling hands into my pockets.

"Two years... and it's the guy you suspected: my coworker."

Math was always my weakest subject I always thought, but now I knew it was reading people. I could not do anything about the latter, so I concentrated on the former. I did not have a calculator, so I processed it aloud.

"If Olivia is close to thirteen months old, and you were pregnant for almost nine months, that would mean you were sleeping with this guy around the time she was conceived." I was going to need a bathroom. I just wasn't sure whether I would puke or defecate first.

As she continued to talk, I was thinking about what I needed to do. First on the list was to get a DNA test on Olivia. Next, my thoughts turned to God. *If You see all and know all, why would You allow this to happen again?*

My feelings toward God deteriorated quickly, but I was also agitated with myself for believing the hype about Him. There was no way He would ever love someone like me, a sinner, and I felt stupid for believing He would.

I was so mad at God that my reaction to Lacey was not what I expected. Frankly, the way I felt made me nervous. I did not get belligerent or raise my voice. I was taking the news all too well.

Having gone through this with my ex-wife, I had an idea of what to expect. Don't get me wrong, it hurt, it hurt bad, But the way I flicked it off like it was no big deal was a clear sign of how messed up I was. In hindsight, I was in shock.

I had no inkling as to how damaged I truly was. When she told the truth and everything came out, I felt like a shaken bottle. At some point real soon, it would open, and the explosion would be of epic proportions.

This is bizarre, but I crawled into bed with her when it was time to go to sleep. *At least she's still with me*, I reasoned. Mentally, I had already checked out, becoming the same traumatized child I had been when Dad died.

The next day things got real from my flawed perspective. Knowing Lacey was at work with the coworker enraged me. I'm sure she told him how much of a pushover I was, and they shared a good laugh at my expense. My paranoia, now heightened, revealed the inadequate feelings lodged deep within me concerning our relationship.

When I got home that night, she felt the need to give me details. That's right, details. I found this odd and felt as though she wanted a reaction out of me, and not a good one.

So many times in the past that I lost count, she threatened to call the cops on me. So much that when Lacey and I would play around, Aubriana would yell, "Mommy, call the cops!" Lacey would end the threat by adding, "When they get here, I'll just tell them to look at your record and then look at mine."

It should have been crystal clear to me that she wanted me to give her a reason to call the police because they had been to the house on two or three occasions. Of course, nothing happened those times other than to expose our girls to our adult idiocy.

She sat on the bed while I stood, arms folded, listening to the details she spat out. By the time she was done, smoke billowed from my ears, and I was exhaling fire, yet I did not react in a volatile way.

In disbelief, I shook my head and mumbled under breath, "I feel like burning this bed." She heard it and sarcastically replied, "You'll have to burn more than just the bed." This was her way of letting me know that the bed was not the only place she and the coworker had been. I took my eyes off the floor and glared at her with disgust. I clearly remember saying to myself, "I'm gonna hurt this girl!"

This was a critical moment. Jesus said, *For out of the abundance of the heart the mouth speaks* (Matthew 12:34b). Therefore, what came out of my mouth started in my heart, then filled my mind, where I allowed it to remain until Satan found an opportune time to trip me into his pit.

She was after a reaction and I had given her one, she just could not hear it. Instead, I returned downstairs, nearly tripping on the tail between my legs.

I, the bottle of emotions, was being shaken with greater intensity. The warning God gave Cain thousands of years ago was echoing in my mind. *Sin is crouching at your door; it desires to have you, but you must rule over it* (Genesis 4:7b NIV). In other words, God was saying, Michael, you're standing on the precipice of a life altering decision. If you look to Me, I will help you escape. If you don't, sin is waiting to swallow you whole.

Shortly after hearing the devastating news and waiting the pending DNA test, I began experiencing discomfort in my chest. When it became more frequent, I went to see a doctor.

He asked a series of questions and handed me a portable EKG like device to strap around my chest. I would wear it for the next twenty-four hours, and it would give a real-time reading of the rhythms of my heart.

With the test results, an analyst noticed some discrepancies and referred me to a cardiologist who would perform an echocardiogram (ultrasound) on my heart. The results showed that I had a "strong heart," which was shocking due to all the cocaine I had done. The doctor believed my heart issues were stress related and advised me to cut out all stress or keep it to a minimum.

All the stress in my life centered on Lacey but cutting her out was not something I was willing to do. Instead, I asked for medication to help cope with the stress. When I learned it would take up to three weeks for the meds to take effect, I panicked. I needed those pills yesterday.

So... I had an epiphany, but only if I could find a drug to hold me over until the meds took effect. Alcohol no longer had a hold on me; cocaine almost killed me, and heroin and I had a falling out. I felt it was time to up the ante, so I threw in the last chip I had, and its name was methamphetamine.

There was no problem getting the drug. Just about all my junkie friends sold it or had some in stock. I made the score, but, after trying it, decided it was not for me. I saw the effect it had on one's teeth and skin. Although, I did not have much to be proud of, the two things I did have were nice teeth and skin, so I continued my search.

In this unholy quest for the mental exodus (besides death), I found a buried treasure. What I discovered would hopefully rebuild my confidence, bolster my self-esteem, make me feel appreciated, and I could take as many doses as my heart would allow. My new drug would be women.

I returned to the bars, searched out who I thought was the prettiest girl and made my move. If they rejected me, so be it. I had no skin in the game. It was all about sex. I never intended to be in a relationship with any of these women. I was already in one. Yes, it was dysfunctional at best, but our relationship banner was still hanging, even if it was by a thread.

Out of all my addictions, women were the worst. I truly have nothing to compare it to. Unlike drugs or booze, getting high on promiscuity never gave me a bloody nose or left me nursing a hangover the next morning. It did, however, eat away at my character as if it was an acidic brew manufactured from the pits of hell. For me to become a good womanizer, I had to deactivate my emotions, drain my morals, and ditch my integrity.

Truth be told, I never understood why these women took interest in me, but I found self-worth in them. Receiving text messages from teachers, doctors, corporate women of America, and even a neurosurgeon from our nation's highest clinic, all wanting to say hello and hear about my day, made me feel like the greatest thing since the iPhone. My ego needed its own social security number. Like Lacey, I too had an excuse to lock my phone and call off work to spend time with these women. Satan had pulled out his strongest tool.

My good persona was short-lived. Many of these women felt demoralized and used once they realized I did not want to be with them long-term. Some were even brought to tears, believing I was *the one*, only to learn later they had been duped. I guess the saying is true, "Hurt people, hurt people."

Thank goodness Granny did not know what I was doing. She would have picked a switch and gone to town on my backside like she had when I was younger. She did not raise me to treat women this way, or anyone else. But what Granny did not know was not important. God knew, (and He controls who gets into His heaven.)

Thirty-four days after submitting to the DNA test, I learned I was in fact Olivia's father. This reignited my desire of becoming a family.

Lacey and I had a long talk and things seemed to improve until an argument flared up out of nowhere. To me, it was fabricated, so I remained calm to see where it was going. It climaxed when Lacey demanded that I leave the house. Having gone through this before with her, I knew that a police officer would force me out if I refused, so I packed an overnight bag and spent the night at my mom's place.

That night I was having a tough time sleeping and in my restless state, decided to return home. I started to leave when Mom, who had fallen asleep on the sofa, heard the jingling of my keys. Once I told her where I was going, she insisted that I not go.

Finally, after much back and forth, she said, "Michael, I'm your mother. You need to listen to me. Don't go!" The desperation in her voice caused me to stutter in my steps outside the door.

Maybe it was her motherly instincts or because she knew her son that she warned me not to go. Probably both.

I hopped in my truck and made my way home. When I pulled onto our street, there was a car I had never seen sitting in the driveway. The shaken bottle that had steadily increased in the pressure of silent rage over the years was at its breaking point. Had I known it would be a long time until I saw Mom again, I would have given her a hug.

CHAPTER EIGHTEEN

SATAN'S SINFUL PUPPET

The shock from seeing the strange vehicle in the driveway left me so angry and confused that my truck ended up parked on the wrong side of the road. As expected, a male exited through the front door. It was my belief the male coworker would be the one. To my surprise, it was an entirely different individual I had not seen before. It did not make me feel any better though. He got into his car and sped off before I could confront him.

Turning my attention back to the house, Lacey was the first thing I saw. She even stepped aside and held the door as I entered as if it were a normal day. The little respect I thought she had for me had only been a mirage. This was not strike one; this was about strike forty-seven, long past a full count.

Even though I was guilty of doing the same thing, seeing the guy made it real. Something I would learn later is that anger is a secondary emotion, triggered by hurt. In my case, her serial cheating hurt me. I wanted get back.

A ton of emotions and scenarios came flooding into my mind, and not one at a time. They came colliding all together. I had never gotten over her past infidelities, having to take a paternity test, the plethora of rude comments she had made. She might have harbored as many complaints about me as far as drugs and booze, but all I kept thinking was, *how could you do this to me?* Gee-whiz, maybe because I was in the middle of a womanizing addiction, but I did not see it that way at the time. My warped thinking led me to believe she was forcing my hand. Was she?

I asked myself, *how many times are you going to let this girl walk all over you?* I went to the bottom of the stairs and looked to see if the girl's door was closed. I wanted answers and did not want them to hear us argue.

Since I have been with more women than this book has pages, I had no right to throw the proverbial first stone, but I claimed the moral high ground; not once did I bring any of these women around our girls. They were my sacred treasure.

Olivia, now eighteen months, rarely slept in her crib. With the side rail removed, she would jump from her crib and into our bed, which was about twelve inches away. When Lacey said the guy she had only known for seven days slept in our bed, is the moment the cork blew.

I remember yelling, "You had him around my kids?", and again, but even louder: "YOU HAD HIM AROUND MY KIDS?" For all the mental posturing I had practiced, always convincing myself I could take the high ground, any control I had left was about to fail.

I yanked her to me and put her in a chokehold. I held on unaware she had lost consciousness until I finally let her go. As she fell to the floor, I instinctively reached out to grab her, but still enraged, withdrew my hand, and watched her fall flat on her face. I was convinced she was getting what she deserved.

Isn't it amazing how one split-second decision can change the trajectory of our lives? To this day, I am haunted by the sound of her nose fracturing on the hardwood floor. It is only for the purpose of this book that I have chosen to relive that awful day.

If my spiritual eyes could have been opened, I'm sure I would have seen Satan and his demons slithering in the corner, applauding my performance. Granny often said, "The devil always leads you into trouble, but he will never lead you out." Ain't that the truth!

As Lacey regained consciousness, I knew the sand in my hourglass of freedom was dwindling fast. I raced to my truck and drove away. I did not know when I would be apprehended, so I called Mom in a panic.

"Mom, I've made a mistake." Before I could go any further, she shouted in terror, "Is she dead?" Maybe she heard the distress in my voice that made her ask that question. I told her what I had done and asked her to go to the house and look after our girls. Thankfully, she did.

The weight of my actions and Mom's reaction took its toll. The ripple effects of my sins would spread far and wide. My major credo had always been that family came first, but my actions, which spoke louder than my words, deemed that to be a fallacy. When push came to shove, I acted like an idiot and lost track of what was most important to me.

I had been to jail several times before, and the thought of going to prison for a long time was something I believed I could not do. I would rather die... and that was the plan... suicide. But before I could execute that plan, I needed to see Granny one last time.

It was barely six in the morning, and she would not be off work for another hour. I arrived at her home and although I could have let myself in, I chose to wait. When her shift ended, I gave her a call. She answered in her usual, bubbly voice but my harried response prompted her to ask what was wrong. I refused to tell her over the phone. I did tell her that I was in town and asked permission to let myself in with the key she had given to me. Access granted.

Like a dog waiting for its owner to come home, I paced back and forth in the front room, juggling the best way to confess my abhorrent behavior.

Finally, Granny arrived. I took her purse and hung up her jacket; she removed her shoes and went into the kitchen to prepare breakfast. In the past, Granny's cooking was a highlight of any of my visits, but this time her hard work meant nothing. The boost in morale I would get from a typical conversation as she made her delicious victuals had zero effect, most probably because it delayed the inevitable, me telling Granny what I had done.

Granny fixed our plates and set them down. She said the blessing over the food. I felt embarrassed and ashamed when she invoked God's name after what I had just done.

When Granny was not laughing or smiling, which was rare, she could be hard to read. This was one of those times. She must have known I would not have been able to speak first, so she began.

"So, what's going on, Grandson?"

I could not look her in the eye, so I stared nervously at my plate, chopping away at my eggs as I explained everything. She was not chewing on her food so much as she was chewing on my words. She responded by saying I needed to own up to my mistakes and, by doing so, I would probably be going to prison.

After cleaning my plate like the good grandson I once was, I stood from the table and gave her a hug. I clinched her tight, maybe tighter than I had ever done before. In my mind, this was not a "see you later" hug. This was a goodbye hug. Granny had always been a constant in my life. The thought of never seeing her again broke me and I sobbed in her arms.

I walked to my truck and turned to see her on the porch. From the time I can remember, she would always step out on the porch or watch from a window and wave as we departed. I cannot describe how the melancholy struck me like lightning. With tears streaming down my face, I blew her a kiss goodbye and drove away.

I know Granny; she would have stood there until I was out of sight and then gone back inside, not to watch TV or talk on the phone, but to talk with God.

I decided a pill overdose would be how I would die. I searched my vehicle for Percocet's prescribed to me from a past surgery. Nothing. I searched for my anxiety medication. Still nothing. Then it hit me… I left them at home.

When a game is on the line and the coach calls the wrong play, what does the quarterback do? He calls an audible, and that is exactly what I did. I stopped at a store where all I could find was extra strength pain medicine. Would it work? I did not know but, I would consume the entire bottle.

I drove to a nearby park and walked into the woods where I could be alone. I collapsed rather than sat on the ground, propping my pitiful self against a large rock. I dumped the pills into my hand, swallowed as many as I could, then repeated the process… until the bottle was empty.

Sitting in a trance like state, I waited. The silence was only interrupted by the rustling of leaves courtesy of two squirrels jumping limb to limb in the trees. For a moment, I was moved by the tranquility of the environment and began to have second thoughts.

After sitting for a while, I began having doubts that the pills would kill me. What would I do? I nearly jumped out of my skin when I heard a voice. I knew this voice and this voice knew me. It was the same voice I heard on the bridge, and it said, "If the pills don't kill you, you can hang yourself from one of these trees." The voice was so real that I looked around to see who was there, but no one was. The dark, sinister voice came from hell.

Hearing those words, I began to cry. The thousands upon thousands of bad choices I had made over the course of thirty-four years all led to this one. The choice before me was the most important I would ever make. If I chose to commit murder by taking my life, I would spend an eternity in a burning hell because I knew better.

Deep down I did not want to die; I wanted to live. I simply hated the life I had been living and the direction it was going. Killing myself would have been the ultimate act of selfishness and betrayal to my daughters and everyone else who loved me.

The park was minutes from Granny's home. She had already lost a son to her next-door neighbor via murder. How would she feel driving past the park her in which her grandson had killed himself? I was still thinking about Michael first, Michael second, and Michael last. God needed my eyes on Him and, until I surrendered, His Spirit would continue to fight for my soul. I began to think about my eternal destiny. I did not want to make a permanent decision based on a temporary problem.

A small ember of hope began to glow inside of me. Could it grow into a full-fledged flame for Him? I could get through this but not on my own. I called Granny and told her what I had done. She phoned my uncle who picked me up and drove me to a hospital.

I walked in on my own accord and told a nurse what I tried to do. She directed me to a room where I changed into a gown and had blood drawn from my arm.

The nurse exited with two vials of blood, then a police officer took her place. This was procedure and was no cause for alarm. When the officer asked for my social security number, my head told me to give a fictitious number, but my tongue did not get the memo. She knew why I was there and offered words of encouragement before leaving.

The next thing I remember is waking to my smiling granny sitting beside me. She had to be running on fumes, but she hid that nicely. The first thing she said was, "I didn't want you to think no one cared, so Granny decided to come down." Mom would join us an hour later.

I kept asking to leave but the nurse insisted I wait until my lab work came back. Finally, after a total of four hours I was discharged. Granny and Mom exited the room, and the nurse pulled the curtain so I could dress.

When I walked out, I was met by an array of security guards and police officers. Out of habit, I turned, locked my fingers behind me, and they handcuffed me on the spot. Being arrested in front of Mom and Granny was an even bigger pill to swallow. I gave them my love before being led away.

In Acts 9:1-9, the author shares an account of the apostle Paul's conversion. Before God transformed Saul into Paul, he was a menace to the church. He went everywhere arresting those who believed in Christ. While on his way to Damascus to arrest more Christians, he was knocked to the ground by a bright light that shown from heaven. The light was so intense that it blinded him for three days. In the midst of this light, Jesus spoke, identified Himself, and then revealed Saul's life purpose.

I give you that account to say this:
When the cops put me into their cruiser, I had no idea that being arrested and sent to jail was the start of my journey to Damascus, that God would meet me along the way, break me, and restore my soul.

CHAPTER NINETEEN

STRAY CATS

We arrived at the station where my handcuffs were removed. An officer walked behind me and directed me to a tiny room where a copy machine, desk, computer, phone, and wooden bench filled the space. This was where I sat.

Putting on a pair of latex gloves and rolling his chair to the copier, the officer said, "We need to take your fingerprints just in case you've committed other crimes we don't know about." His condescending tone made me want to put my fingerprints across his *Shirley Temple.*

After fingerprinting my digits and palms, next was the mugshot. In the very first mugshot I had ever taken, I smiled. The photographing officer on that occasion yelled to a coworker, "Hey, Larry, this guy's smiling. I think he enjoys being here!" I made a point this time not to smile. I also felt the regret of being a repeat customer.

I prepared for what I thought was to come when the officer

threw a curveball. He opened a drawer and pulled out two cotton swabs. "Open your mouth."

"What for? I never did this in the past."

"That's because you've never been arrested on felony charges, now *open your mouth*."

This was a horse of an entirely different color. My apprehension for what was coming drove the drowsiness from the pills away. I would not be staying in their jail because felony charges meant felony court. I would be taking a ride to a different jail, the big boy jail.

I was transferred to Summit County Jail and frisked for a second time. A deputy pointed to a four-foot by four-foot steel plate and instructed me to stand on it, while he stared at a computer screen. This device would scan my body for concealed contraband such as drugs and weapons.

All five of my tattoos were photographed for gang affiliation purposes, and there was one more mugshot to which to submit. (Submit, a simple word really. I thought I knew its meaning but God would grant me the supernatural association of the word.)

I was given brown sandals, an orange jumpsuit, and then called to a table where a caseworker would review my mental and physical health records. Considering all I had been through within the past twenty-four hours, my mental stability was nothing more than fragile.

The caseworker verified I was on a 50mg dose of anxiety and depression medication and recommended I continue taking it while in their custody (this dose would climb to 150mg before I left the jail).

With the booking process complete, I was given a free call

before I was sent to a housing unit. Living in the cellphone generation, the only number I had committed to memory was Mom's, so I gave her the call. Her verbal lashing only worsened my frame of mind. *Should have seen that comin'.* With the call going nowhere, I ended it and joined a single-file line of a dozen offenders and began my walk of shame.

Our first stop was a laundry room where we each were handed one of the following: three-inch toothbrush, three-inch tube of toothpaste, small blanket, bed sheet, coffee mug (pre-stained), thin bar of soap, face cloth, body towel, and "Maximum-Security" deodorant (some would call, instead, "odorant").

I looked over the gray blanket and noticed long, blonde hairs laced in the stitching. *If this is their idea of clean, I can only imagine what everything else looks like.*

With the bare necessities in hand, we continued our walk. The line dwindled at every stop because we would let someone off at their living unit. Men already inside would stare at us as if we were filet mignon steaks and they were ravenous lions. It was nerve-racking to say the least, but I kept a tough exterior as best I could.

Finally, a thick metal door, which seemed to be nothing but flaky paint and rust, buzzed, and I stepped timorously into the lion's den. I felt like a new kid who walked into class after it had already started. All eyes were on me, but I did not return any of their gazes. The only *good* thing about my situation, if you could call it that, was violent offenders were given their own cell. I would not have to worry about living with anyone else... yet.

The unit, or "block" as it is called on the inside, had twenty-six cells, thirteen on the top floor, thirteen on the main floor. In the middle and on both floors were two showers, each filthier than the next.

I marched up to cell twenty-three and placed my belongings on the writing table. The suction from the door opening circulated dust bunnies adorning the floor. My attention immediately went to the writing on the walls from past occupants. Some were inspirational but most were angry tirades, crude ramblings, and emotional epithets.

My first objective was to give the room a thorough cleaning. Although I kept my eyes to myself on the way in, I did spot a utility closet full of supplies next to the showers. I was careful not to erase any of the graphite-laced wallpaper. It was a written reminder of the pain and mental torment others before me had endured. I even contemplated adding a few lines of grief to the graffiti.

A panel in the hallway, only used during count-time, controlled cell doors in the block. Count-time is when all offenders are locked in their cells and a deputy or corrections officer (CO) counts every offender. This happens three times a day to ensure everyone is accounted for.

As day turned to night, I laid there with nothing but my thoughts to keep me company. This was the first time I had to ponder the events of the day. In a sick twist of logic, I was relieved to be in jail. Had I not been arrested at the hospital; I may have been tempted to run or finish my life for real.

The how's and why's circulated in my mind, but I failed to come up with any valid answers. How did I end up here? Why didn't I heed Mom's warning not to return home? Why did God let this happen? These unanswered questions fueled my anger. In the end, in the quietest of the night, after I sorted through these things, all roads led back to God. He was to blame.

I did not regret what I had done. My only regret was getting caught. I kept thinking *if I had only kept her from falling...* What I should have been thinking was had I never put my hands on her, I would still be free. If God's goal was to change my warped way of thinking, He had His work cut out for Him.

Somehow, through sheer exhaustion, I dozed off, too soon to be awakened by the bellowing of a deputy, "TRAYS GENTLEMEN!" This was the battle cry for the three meals we were fed each day.

Our food was brought inside the block, and we lined up in a disorganized chow line, which was not a chow line all time.

That morning, breakfast consisted of one perfectly square flavorless biscuit, a plastic pack of peanut butter, and two pieces of bread. Looking at this pitiful excuse of a meal confirmed what I knew to be true; this was going to be a hard grind.

Later that day, I was taken down the hall to video court where I heard my charges and received a reasonable bond. I had a fighting chance of meeting it. I just needed to call home and plan.

Certain offenders controlled the phones in the block, but, since I was the "quiet guy," I was given access to one. Granny's number reappeared in my memory, so I called her collect. I felt bad for sticking her with the charges, but if I could get a message to her, she could relay it to Mom and my siblings.

Granny's approach was not what I expected. She attacked me with love and encouraged me to devote some of my time talking to God. Before the timed call ended, she prayed and asked God to protect me and to let me feel His love. That's what I loved about Granny, she always stayed plugged into heaven's switchboard.

A few weeks later, I was indicted and could not believe the charges. I did not know that the State often over-indicts as a scare-tactic to increase the chances of a defendant taking a plea deal (this is my personal belief). Because I was not privy to their schemes, I called Mom, boiling with anger and disbelief. I blamed everyone from Lacey to the legal system for what I was going through.

At a certain point Mom had heard enough. She interrupted, and said, "Mike, *stop* looking at everyone else and *start* focusing on the part you played in the situation." This was a stance she would take often during our calls, rightfully so, but worrying about the part I played would have to wait. Making bail was my number one priority.

I broke my word of keeping to myself and began talking to some of the men in the block. One of the first things most of these guys would do is offer legal advice. Who knew there were so many *lawyers* locked up? They offered advice from their flawed perspective, and then pointed me to others in the block who could help on specifics.

All this moving from one person to the next almost made me dizzy and put me in front of people I should have avoided. Many times, these people were troublemakers, did not know what they were talking about, or tried to help only to learn my business.

Gang activity ran wild in the jail. I cannot begin to number how many times we were ordered to "LOCK IT DOWN" (return to your cell and close the door) because of a fight in our unit or another nearby. Seeing staff sprint down the hall at a moment's notice became the norm.

The gangs in our block controlled everything except the air that flowed into your lungs, and on some days that was even up for discussion. They ran a store, which is technically illegal and frowned upon by staff, but is vital to the offender economy.

Whoever in the gang was running the block would also send someone (aka crash dummy) to distract any worker or offender while his gang stole from vacant cells or from the offender himself. On several occasions I witnessed stabbings and beatings, some of them too close for comfort.

I was talking to a man on the top floor when a gang member ran up and punched him in the face. When he turned to retaliate, I was almost doused in the blood coming from his cheek. When the deputies rushed up the stairs, the man who threw the first punch tossed the shank (stabbing knife shaved into a weapon) he had used to puncture the other man's cheek.

After a few more incidents like this, I quickly became anesthetized to the violence and other things that are typical in jail. I also learned you would have to be a fool not to always be on guard.

It was rare for a gang member to be alone, and if they were, the consequences could be fatal. For example, I had just locked down one evening when a scuffle involving four men broke out in front of my door. From the window, I watched men from the same gang circling a lone rival gang member. Like evil hyenas howling, these gang members mocked him before beating him like an egg. When they split his head, I could no longer watch.

I returned to my bed and sat quietly, listening to them slam the man repeatedly into my door. I wondered how in the world my life had gotten to this point and how human beings could do this to one another. It was chaos and anarchy in its purest form. I was asked multiple times to join different gangs. I always declined.

Tension in the block was perpetually thick as mud. One wrong word or phrase could set off a jail type nuclear war. Something as simple as a gang finding out you were from a city other than theirs could result in an all-out brawl and, of course, all members were expected to represent their hood.

The dreaded day finally came when I was approached. "Parker, what city are you from?" I did not know what to tell them, so I stuck with the truth. "I was born in Cleveland but raised in

Akron." To my surprise, being from both cities granted me some type of mystical immunity. Who would have known that something I had no control over, my place of birth, would help keep me safe in jail? Or was it the angel of the Lord who shut the mouths of the lions on my behalf (see Daniel 6:22)?

About one-third of the men in our block were brought into the jail under the influence of drugs. The legal issues each of them dealt with were compounded by the withdrawals with which there were wrestling. Seeing grown men cry and listening to them moan in pain as their bodies craved the drug they no longer had access to can be summed up in one word. Sad.

For the life of me, I could not figure out why I was having so much trouble making bail. I had the assets to pay the bondsman but could not get anyone to follow through. I was at wits end, and the drama around me was brewing into a storm Noah would have loved. I would learn later that God was honoring my Granny's prayers of not releasing me until He was ready.

The whole getting out on bond issue was all I could think about, so God grabbed my attention in a way I did not see coming. It started when two men came to my cell. Not knowing what to expect, I stood poised to defend myself.

"Hang on!" one demanded, raising his hands into the air. "We have a question about the Bible, and someone sent us to you." I did not believe them. Why come to me? I was not going around talking about God. In fact, I did my best not to think about Him let alone speak about Him. There was no reason for them to link the two of us together; and, if my intuition was right, I did not want trapped in a cell with the scales tipped in their favor.

I listened to their question and knew exactly where to locate the answer. Before sharing, though, I led them to a table away from my cell. I did not want to risk them loitering around because of the trepidation I had toward God talk.

I opened their Bible and brought attention to several verses. Witnessing a metaphorical lightbulb turn on, seemingly for the first time, was unforgettable. Before I allowed myself to be sucked in any further, I retreated to my cell, but the indescribable feeling of knowing I had helped someone was overwhelming.

What transpired should have been expected. We all know what happens when you feed a stray cat, right? It shows up when you least expect it, seeking more and more food, and, before you know it, it's your cat. Well, this is what these *cats* did, return for more spiritual food.

I hunkered down in the cell hoping they would get the hint, but they didn't. Although I was no longer worried about their motives, I would only talk to them from inside the cell while they listened from the outside. When I would not come out, they brought chairs and Bibles and sat in my doorway.

It was everything I did *not* want. God seemed to be saying, *you're not getting away from Me that easy.* Even though I betrayed Him with my false promise during that drug-addled night, when I needed Him the most He was still there.

As much as I tried not to get involved, the joy I received from helping people extinguished those efforts. Perhaps it was my hubris instead of a true willingness to do God's will, but at least I was doing something. There was no way I would send these cats away hungry.

Not every answer came easily. I had to dig into the Word to pull out its buried treasure. Take it from me; it is impossible to study the Bible and not become infected by its truth. I spent many years trying to fight off the virulent virus.

Something I often share with people is "Get into God's Word

and God's Word will get into you." I've learned this through life experiences, both good and bad. Oftentimes, He works on us the most during our bad times. God was dealing with my heart in a way He saw fit, and sometimes I threw a fit the way He saw it.

Here's the thing: my issues were rooted in the fact that I was convinced God did not love me. I believed the words of John 3:16, *For God so loved the world that He gave His only begotten Son, that whoever believes in Him should not perish but have everlasting life*, but I felt excluded from this promise.

Over the next few weeks our Bible study group of three multiplied by four. Someone suggested we do a study on the End Times, and I offered to take it. Not wanting to do a disservice to the subject, I spent much of the week in preparation for what I felt would be a great spiritual adventure.

The book of Revelation can be hard to understand so I decided to present it in story form. I created fictitious characters and sprinkled the story with Scripture to validate its points. I was blown away at how quickly it took shape. I presented it to the guys, and they were admittedly affected. This became my first crude yet unpublished piece of literature that lays in the bottom of my writing drawer.

This novelette, which I hope to publish, titled, *Will You Be Ready* took on a life of its own.

Soon afterwards, a man came knocking on my door. He had heard about *Will You Be Ready* and asked me to read it. Because it was my only copy, I begrudgingly agreed. When the doors opened after count-time, he was at my door knocking. With a somber look, he asked, "Is this stuff really going to happen?"

"Yes," I answered, "according to Bible it's all going to happen,"

His interest was for good reason, I found out later. He confessed to being Muslim. While this surprised me, he went on to say that reading my story helped open his heart to Christ. I gave the papers back to him and insisted he jot down every scripture so he could read them for himself.

Over the next couple days, when he saw me, he would ask, "Do you have any more chapters?" Not only was I pleased to see his interest in Christ growing, but it also gave me more fuel to continue writing.

On the third day, I went to his cell with the latest chapters. His cell was empty. He had been released, and his sudden departure saddened me greatly. No matter how it spun in my head, I knew this was no chance encounter. This account, and many unwritten here, opened my heart toward service.

I sensed God calling me in some fashion, and the thought frightened me. Still in my anti-God mind frame, as far as I was concerned, He could call someone else. I was used to pleasing myself and helping others is such a selfless act. Working for God meant He would be my boss; and, if I got my way, which I usually did, that would never happen. Yes, His benefits are out of this world (pun intended) but I was convinced God did not love me. I refused to subject myself to His abuse daily.

To get Him off my back, I made God a deal; the same deal I made when I faced prison years before. If He would allow me to post bail, I would do His will, and if I didn't, He could take my freedom. In hindsight, I had no clue what I was saying and strongly advise you to be careful what you say, especially to God, because words have power!

Two long arduous weeks after making this vow, and after three months of misery, I was released on bond. Having put forth no effort into becoming a better person, and still at odds with God, I walked out of jail the same way I entered, a tangled mess. God, however, placed a desire to help others inside me for what would later prove to be a divine purpose.

CHAPTER TWENTY

GOD HAS A PLAN

I thought I had everything under control. I pushed aside support from family and friends to do the right thing. This pride, stubbornness, and going back to what got me locked up in the first place landed me back in jail seven days later, with additional charges.

Before posting bond, prison was just an option. Having done what I did while out on bond, prison was the only expected outcome. The topic of discussion now with my court appointed attorney was not guilt or innocence, but the length of my sentence.

In the seven days I was out on bond, the jail had experienced an influx of offenders, and the overcrowding resulted in no vacant cells. My new home would be on a cot in front of the showers. This was the worst spot in the entire block because it left me vulnerable on every side. Imagine trying to sleep on the floor in the middle of a shopping mall. This is what the flow of our block was like, but it resembled an insane asylum much more closely than a suburban shopping mall.

Everything this time around was significantly worse: the violence, staff, offenders, drugs. To compound things, the new block I was housed in seemed to be the headquarters for every gang on the East Coast.

Over the next few months, I managed to fly under the radar, but that changed when I made a life changing decision.

It was a Monday morning when I was awakened by a deputy who said the church service I had signed up for was about to begin. Here's the thing: *I had not signed up for anything.* I started to tell him; but realizing attending would get me out of the insanity of the block, I nodded and went with him.

There were twenty-three of us in the service, and our guest speakers were two older men, one who had previously served time. They opened the service by singing a simple song I sang thousands of times as a child, *Jesus Loves Me*, but on this day it resonated within me.

Throughout the service, one of the guest speakers kept looking at me. He did not say a word, just smiled. The Holy Spirit was chiseling a path to my heart, and I did not even know it. It was so subtle. I started to feel ashamed for the way I had treated God, whereas before I did not care.

As the service closed, they led us in "Jesus Loves Me" for the final time. I could not hold back the tears. Don't ask me how, but in that moment, I knew with my whole heart that Jesus *does* love me.

Only the Holy Spirit could have orchestrated what happened next. The smiling guest walked over, put his arm around me, and whispered, "You're ready, aren't you? I can see the Holy Spirit is dealing with you. Jesus loves you so much that He died on a cross for you." We prayed together and I rededicated my life to Christ.

I have always had a vivid imagination, as a child and still do. The day in jail when I stopped running from Christ, I imagined my guardian angel collapsing to the floor and saying, *finally* as he wiped decades of sweat from his brow. I had definitely kept him busy.

When I backslid after my overdose, it started a chain reaction, neglecting daily prayer and Bible reading being the first causalities. Missing a few days here and there seemed small. Eventually, it damaged my relationship with God as those few days became a few weeks and then a few months.

If Satan would have appeared before me and tried taking the Bible out of my hands, I would have been defensive and pulled back. Instead, he placed small distractions along my way to loosen my grip until it weakened enough that I lost my grip altogether. I was determined not to skip over the small stuff because it's the little things that can add up and cause the most trouble (see Song of Songs 2:15).

Before returning to the block, I accepted a Bible from the smiling guest. I could not wait to get back and use the quietness of offenders sleeping to be with the Lord. I was spiritually malnourished, and the Holy Spirit put such a hunger for the Word inside me that no matter how much He fed me, I hungered for more.

Since my return to jail, I had not faced any opposition from any offenders; but now that Christ was running my life, it put a huge target on my back.

An incident occurred when I befriended Armando. Armando was small, had tattoos on his face and energy to burn. He slept on a cot below me on the first floor. Fully aware that all I read was biblical material, he would often ask for something to read during count-times.

One night, Armando came upstairs and brought four of his friends. One stood at the top of the east and west stairwells. The other two stood on the side of my cot, about ten feet away.

This was red flag number one. Red flag number two came when Armando sat at a nearby chess table, set up the pieces in the wrong formation, and called me over to play. He did not play chess (I knew this), which was a dead giveaway that something was fishy.

"What's up, man?" I probed, refusing to sit.

"Listen, I heard you got some commissary" (food items).

"Go on."

"Dude's around here is hungry," he said with no eye contact.

I looked at the men, and unlike the chess pieces, they were positioned perfectly. Our deputies would see every move.

I fixed my gaze back on Armando. "Wait a minute! Just because I have a few things you expect me to feed the entire block?"

He rambled on. "I'm just sayin'. You ain't got no coffee, no Ramen Noodles, no nothin'?

"Man, I aint got nothin' for you!" I barked back, shaking my head in disbelief.

"Okay, well I know you been good to me but I gotta stick wit' my dudes."

I was flabbergasted. Armando, whom I considered a friend, was trying to extort me. Obviously, my kindness meant nothing to him.

I felt the anger of God rise within me and slammed by fist on the table, knocking over the game pieces. "Okay, cool!" I retorted.

Just as I uttered those words, a deputy yelled, "LOCK IT DOWN!" and everyone dispersed to his own cell. I noticed the clock read 6:15 p.m. and lockdown was not until 9 p.m. I thought it was strange because no one was fighting, and we were not short-staffed. For whatever reason, though, the deputy took his chair into the hall and remained there until the end of his shift.

As I lay on the cot, I pondered the seriousness of the situation as it slowly started to sink in. I knew when the doors opened, the possibilities of me drinking my peanut butter sandwich through a straw for breakfast was extremely high.

In my mind's eye, the faces of the four men appeared alongside Armando's face. That is when I realized they were all in the same gang. It was hard to comprehend. I was on the verge of a serious butt whoopin' over a few ramen noodles and half a bag of generic coffee. In my most dire moments, I have always asked God for help. He always answered even though it might not have been what I wanted. Once again, I went to The Well and said aloud, "Lord, You have got to help me! There is no way I can handle this on my own!", and I prayed desperately.

Straightway my mind went to King David. If there was anyone in the Bible who was plotted against numerous times, it was him. A nudge from the Holy Spirit sent me to the book of Psalm. I thumbed through it and came to chapter 40:13-15 (NIV).

Be pleased to save me, Lord; come quickly, Lord, to help me. May all who want to take my life be put to shame and confusion; may all who desire my ruin be turned back in disgrace. May all who say to me, 'Aha! Aha!' be appalled at their own shame.

I sensed the Holy Spirit telling me to read on so I flipped back until I came to Psalm 38:12,19-22 (NIV).

Those who want to kill me set their traps, those who would harm me talk of my ruin; all day long they scheme and lie... Many have become my enemies without cause; those who hate me without reason are numerous. Those who repay my good with evil lodge accusations against me, though I only seek to do what is good. Lord, do not forsake me; do not be far from me, my God. Come quickly to help me, my Lord and my Savior.

I read this aloud as a prayer to God until a calming peace washed over me.

I could hear loud yelling throughout the block when the doors were unlocked the next morning. I went to get my breakfast tray; and, on the way, walked past a cell from where the yelling had come. Hearing my name, I backed up and saw the leader of the gang standing on a bed, shouting at nine guys, Armando, the four who were with him yesterday, and four more guys. The original group of five I thought I was going to have a problem with had doubled. Just when I thought things could not get worse, the man on the bed said, "Parker is a good dude! Leave him alone!" I got out of there before they saw me, but it was enough to make me breathe a deep sigh of relief and an audible, "Thank You, Jesus!"

God used this situation to teach me the importance of trusting in Him. After all, at the core of every good relationship is trust. Psalm 18:30b says, "He is a shield to all who trust in Him" and God honored His Word.

Before the day ended, several gang members approached me, shook my hand, and apologized. These were the same men I watched stomp out other offenders, literally. Only God could have fought this battle for me.

A verse I clung to during my incarceration was Psalm 34:7 (NIV), *The angel of the Lord encamps all around those who fear Him, And delivers them.* If you belong to Christ, this promise belongs to you.

By now, I had been in the county jail for seven months, and sentencing day was approaching fast. I was enjoying the sanctity of my new cell by praying, having one on one Bible studies, and encouraging those who needed encouraged. It's amazing how much time flies when you stop focusing on *your* needs and start focusing on the needs of *others*.

I was concerned about sentencing, but not consumed with it. According to my attorney, there were a few things working in my favor: I had never been to prison, had a spotless juvenile record, and never had a felony.

The state also ordered a pre-sentence investigation, which is an interview between a caseworker and offender. My caseworker told me their recommendation to the court would be anger management treatment instead of prison.

In preparation for court, a fellow offender and I prayed and fasted, seeking God's will. When the judges gavel went down to close the court proceedings, I went down with it. He sentenced me to the maximum I could receive, five years.

Initially, I took it in stride; but as time went on, it began to sink in. I returned to my single man cell, closed the door, and knelt to pray... but I couldn't. I sat on the bed to read my Bible... but I couldn't. Finally, out of total despair, I held the Bible above my head, seconds from hurling it into the toilet, instead slamming it on the table.

Never in my life have I felt as alone as I did in that moment. Whenever I faced a tragedy, I always had someone to talk to, but there in that dark, dingy cell I had no one. Part of me wanted to believe God still had it out for me but I refused to let the thought take root. For once, I was not mad at God, only at the outcome of that day in court.

I felt the warmth of tears slowly trickle down my face as I sat, not knowing what to do. I don't know why I put my hands over my heart, but I did as a desperate plea came from the depths of my soul. "God, I need You to talk to me. I feel like You have abandoned me!", then fell back on the bed and sobbed.

What happened next reminds me of a child who scraped their knee. Before the parent can administer aid, they need to calm the child. I believe this is how our heavenly Father is with us.

Once I regained composure, I reached for my Bible. When I opened it, the only verse highlighted jumped off the page:

*For I know the plans I have for you,' declares the Lord, 'plans to prosper you and not to harm you, plans to give you hope and a future. (*Jeremiah 29:11 NIV).

The tears began to flow again, but this time they were tears of joy, tears of relief. I had heard from God. He met me on my road to Damascus and spoke to me directly. When I needed Him the most He was there. All I had to do was call on His name.

Most of my life I believed God was against me when the only thing He wanted to do was love me. The years I spent running from Him were for naught. He was by my side and going nowhere. I get emotional thinking about it now.

I had no idea what it was, but God was sending me to prison for a divine purpose. There were those who were shocked by my sentence. God was not. He was in control the whole time; and, when God is in control, nothing is ever out of control.

After reading Jeremiah 29:11, I got on my knees to worship the Lord and had the strangest sensation. It was as if someone had placed a warm blanket around me. The peace of God rushed in and enveloped my innermost being. All I could do was cry in His presence. It was such a sacred experience; one I will never forget.

Days before I transferred to prison, a deputy called me into the hall. Waiting there was a staff member who had been watching me over the past few months. She had noticed I was a follower of Christ and wanted to give me a couple books before I left. I thanked her for the kind gesture and returned to my cell.

I casually opened the first book and found a three-page handwritten letter inside. In it, she expressed how much of an impact I had made on her life and marveled at how I was able to keep a cheerful outlook despite my environment and circumstances. The last four words in the letter made me cry, "You give me hope!"

There I was in an orange jumpsuit, facing the worst time in my life, about to serve a nickel in the penitentiary, and *I* gave them hope. No. All the credit goes to my Lord and Savior, Jesus Christ. The light He shown *on* me was now shining *through* me for all to see. To God be the glory!

CHAPTER TWENTY-ONE

INSIDE THE WALLS

The prison doors slammed shut. I was on my own. Inside were men from all levels of society who had collectively committed just about every sin under the sun. However, that did not prohibit the power of God from scaling the fences and breaching the walls to enter the hearts of those willing to accept Him.

There would be new realities to face and fresh problems to deal with. This was *not* County Jail. Men who were emotionally bankrupt and institutionalized by the system would now be my neighbors.

I would see the most creative and talented men do things I could only dream about doing. I would see a sea of fathers who represented a family out of alignment due to his absence, fathers who brought tears to the eyes of their children by not being present in their lives. I would see anguish on the faces of men who had lost a loved one and could not be with their family to grieve. I would also see men cry tears of joy as they humbled themselves before Almighty God after giving Him their heart.

To me, these men were more than a number on a badge; they were my family. I am convinced that one of the reasons God allowed my entry to prison, apart from growing closer to Him, was to not only see a need but to feel it as well. Being forced to wear a state uniform and told when to eat and sleep is drastically different from putting clothes on by choice, clocking in and out at work, then returning home at the end of the day.

Over the next few years, the greatest Teacher the world has ever known, the Holy Spirit, would school me. Throughout my life, He sought to teach me, but I was notorious for cutting class. The Holy Spirit would teach me about myself and more about God in these wretched surroundings than I ever would have learned as a free man.

Prison was where God would place my feet on a path to my life purpose. Believe me when I say it was not easy. There was a lot of stubbornness in me. I needed broken down to the smallest molecule so He could rebuild me into a vessel of His design.

On the surface, it seemed as though my life was ruined but I found peace in the promise of Romans 8:28, *And we know that all things work together for the good of those who love God, and to those who are called according to His purpose.*

God has a unique way of turning what we consider the lemons in our lives into lemonade. Yes, at times His squeezing process can be brutal, but rest assured it is for our benefit and His glory.

I am truly humbled to be your guide as we journey across the prison yard together. Stay close and pay special attention to each account you read. Although our circumstances may differ, I am confident you will relate to something.

I have chosen not to focus on the perversions, perils, and peccadilloes of prison. I would much rather share how God took the ashes of my life and exchanged them for His beauty, while touching lives along the way.

CHAPTER TWENTY-TWO

GOD WILL PROVIDE

And my God shall supply all your need according to His riches in glory by Christ Jesus. Philippians 4:19

Before we received state uniforms, we were strip-searched. One by one we were ordered to squat, bend, lift, and cough (this is also required before and after visits from family and friends). When it was not your turn, you were to plant your palms on a wall and face forward. On this occasion, the CO began to laugh. Unable to turn around and see what was going on made things even more awkward.

Several other COs came over, joined the laughter as one of them shouted, "DEAD MAN WALKING!" That's when I realized what they were doing. They were mocking Tim, the man on death row whom I met in county jail. U.S. Marshals were escorting him across the yard, and it was creating a stir. Anytime a death row offender was moved, the entire compound had to be shut down. They wanted no interaction between general population offenders and death row offenders.

Had it been anywhere else, I would have spoken up for Tim and taken some of the heat. This was no place, however, to make waves, even if it was the humane thing to do.

After the search, I dressed into a uniform and was sent to a temporary cell where another offender like me was waiting. The only items in the cell: a bunk bed, sink, toilet, and the bruised Bible I received from the smiling guest in County Jail.

My cellmate asked to read it, and I agreed but only if he read aloud. This was my way of discussing the Lord with him. The way he took to the Bible, I knew in my heart he would be leaving with it. Though a bittersweet moment, he would have something to read and grow in the Lord, and it would leave me with nothing.

Since he arrived before me, he was the first to leave. He gathered his belongings and, before he could ask, I handed him the Bible. We prayed together, then he left. I was now alone and without a Bible. If anyone knew how much I needed one, it was God. I prayed about it and left it in His capable hands.

It was about four days after I started praying that an offender pulled me aside. "God told me to give you this," the man said. Having heard people speak for God most of my life, I was hesitant to even talk to him. I did not know him from Adam, and myself being only a few days old in prison, I did not know if this was some type of shenanigan. I took the book, thanked him, and kept it movin'.

Once in the cell, I noticed it was not just a book but *The Book*. I examined it more closely and saw it was a Thompson Chain Reference Bible, what I considered the Bugatti of Bibles. It just so happened to be the exact style Bible gifted to me thirteen years prior for my first missionary trip to South Africa. I had misplaced it during my divorce and never saw it again.

What I find amazing is the conversation Granny and I had days before I left at prison. I explained how the Bible I had was in bad shape and would not last the duration of my five-year sentence. Naturally, she offered to purchase a new one. She had just retired, and I did not want to put that financial burden on her. I suggested we wait until I got to prison before doing anything.

As I marveled at my new Bible, I opened it and found this handwritten message written on its sleeve.

"To a Man of God: I would like to sow this Bible into your life. I call you blessed and prosperous on this journey we call LIFE. May you come to know who you are more and more in Christ! May these words become who you are; As He is, so are to you be to all you come in contact with. BE THE LIGHT!
~ Joseph Gray."

Joe would become one of my closest friends in prison. His role as a mentor was the perfect position for him as it was a blessing for me to have met him. He was a believer in Christ and full of faith. God would use him to whoop me into spiritual shape. Countless others had tried but I would not sit still long enough to listen. Now that I was in prison, the Holy Spirit was teaching me to *be still* and know that God is God (Psalm 46:10).

As it would turn out, the Bible Joe gave me had been gifted to him. He already had one he favored, so the gifted Bible sat on his desk for several months. In my heart, I believe God set it aside for me.

CHAPTER TWENTY-THREE

YOU MATTER TO GOD

But even the very hairs of your head are all numbered.
Luke 12:7

Prison can be a dark and lonely place. It takes little to no effort to seep into one's feelings. I was now in a permanent cell and had a new bunkie (cellmate). It was a relief to learn we would get along. Much of the stress a person could feel in prison can arise from having a bad bunkie.

Chow was now in a cafeteria. Going was mandatory, eating was not. The first few days I walked with my bunkie and his friend. It was nice to have someone to talk with. That changed when we returned to the cell, and he told me to find someone else to hang out with. While he never told me so, I believed he did not want to be seen with me because he had made comments about me being a square (lame). This rejection triggered issues I had felt my entire life. Maybe it was worse because it was an offender shunning me. Regardless, hearing this made me feel alone. A dark depression set in.

I stayed in contact with Mom and Granny by way of phone calls and letters, but I never heard from my siblings unless I initiated contact. It made me feel like an afterthought or an asterisk in the book of my family lore, which drove me deeper into depression. I had my share of issues but did not think I was a bad brother. As it would turn out, I would not see my siblings at all during my five years of incarceration.

One evening, I was venting to my bunkie (inside the cell of course) and he began to shake his head.

"You just don't get it."

His remark stopped me cold. "Get what?" I questioned.

"Your family don't care nothin' about you."

Unsure of how to reply, I remained silent, but his words stuck. They swirled about in my head for a few minutes but, no matter, the hurt lingered. I don't blame him for what he said. He was simply replying honestly to the frustration I was putting into the ether.

Sometime later, the chaplain announced there would be a family day. I signed up and ran back to call Mom (technically, running is forbidden except in the recreation yard or in the gymnasium. Let's just say I walked with purpose).

I was ecstatic when she agreed to come. It had been a long time since we had seen one another, and I looked forward to spending time together.

The day of the event, I woke feeling like a kid on Christmas morning. I ironed my clothes, put on some "smell good" (scented oil) and was ready to carpe diem. I was going to see

Mom.

An hour before it started, I called to make sure she had the correct address, proper ID, and all the other particulars. The metaphorical party balloons I held marked *Anticipation* exploded. The ones marked *Forgotten, Alone,* and *Depression* swelled to maximum capacity when she told me she would not be attending.

In prison, there isn't much to look forward to on any given day. Being able to see my family was the next best thing to being released! I dreamed of moments like these. (I know what you're thinking; had I not gone to prison, I wouldn't have been in this predicament, right.)

I almost decided not to go until a friend offered to share his mom with me. I had seen his parents before, so she wasn't a total stranger, but we had never met.

About one hundred of us offenders filed into the gymnasium. I stood back and watched them embrace their loved ones, hoping Mom would suddenly appear. It never happened. I won't sugarcoat it; I would need to muster up every ounce of strength within me to make it through the event.

As I stood alone, my friend summoned me over and introduced me to Jean, his mother. Right away, I noticed how accepting and loving she was of me. The love of God that poured from her pores reminded me of Granny, making our time extra special. Being in such a dark place as prison, recognizing the Spirit of God is almost automatic.

Jean sat between her son and me as we joined in singing old church songs together. If you would have walked by, you would have thought we had been friends for years. She made me feel special in a way that I had not experienced in many years. It really affected me, in a positive way.

When it came time to leave, I thanked her for allowing me to be part of her day with her son. A few tears of mine doused her shirt collar when we said our goodbyes. I had no idea the role Jean would play in my future. God had preordained our meeting.

Before returning to the block, we were strip-searched for a second time, as is the norm, but I was so mentally occupied with Mom's absence that I did not let it dehumanize me. All I felt compelled to do was get back to the cell and talk with God.

I did not recognize it then, but my desire to talk with God was a sign I was growing in relationship with Him. It was a big step to think of God first. He was changing my heart as He drew me closer to Him (see James 4:8).

When I got back, I was able to be alone. I climbed on the bunk and covered my head with a blanket to shield my tears. Every emotion I had hidden below the surface came out in muffled sobs, missing my daughters, not seeing my family, meeting Jean, the pain of feeling alone and forgotten. Emptying my soul and tear ducts, I lamented and told God all that was on my heart.

When I recovered, I noticed how the sun shone brightly outside the window. Pushing myself up, I saw a flock of sparrows sunbathing in the grass where the rays ended. Instantly, the Holy Spirit reminded me of the words of Jesus, and I grabbed my Bible.

Luke 12:6,7 (NIV) *Are not five sparrows sold for two pennies? Yet not one of them is forgotten by God. Indeed, the very hairs of your head are all numbered. Don't be afraid; you are worth more than many sparrows.*

Again, God spoke to me from His Word. Matthew 10:29 tells us not a single sparrow can die without God knowing. So, if God attends the funeral of a single bird, and He says we are more valuable than many birds, then His love for us cannot be measured.

Desiring to be liked, accepted, and loved is not necessarily a bad thing; but, at the end of the day, what others think about you doesn't matter. What matters is what God says about you in His Word, and He says you are *priceless!*

Take courage. God sees you and has a personalized plan for your life regardless of your age, surroundings, or situation you may have gotten yourself into. Right now, at this very moment, *YOU MATTER TO GOD!*

CHAPTER TWENTY-FOUR

FORGIVEN

Then He said to her, Your sins are forgiven. Luke 7:48

After much prayer, I decided to stay at LORCI and become a cadre instead of riding out to another prison. A cadre is someone who maintains the prison at intake facilities. I moved into the cadre block and out of the general population block. This meant I would have a new bunkie.

Since I was a first timer, I barely knew any of the slang used in prison. A term I heard often was given to offenders who committed sexual acts against children. Staff used this derogatory term as well. Unbeknownst to me, my new bunkie had this term bestowed upon him.

To be able to understand prison, you must understand the hierarchy. Murderers would say child molesters are the worst; child molesters would say murderers are the worst. Other sexual crimes are third. The rest really aren't talked about unless their crime was heinous.

I could tell my new bunkie loved to talk because he would not stop talking. I was tired and ready to unpack, but there was one thing he needed to get off his chest. "I want to let you know that

I *do* have a sex case," he said.

I paused to gather my thoughts. "Well... have you asked God to forgive you?"

"Yes, I have," he fired back.

"Then who am I to hold it against you?"

This was the only time we spoke about it. He respected me and I respected him. Not many saw it my way. I understood why he stayed in the cell when he was not working. The men in the block verbally disemboweled him whenever they had a chance. The minute his shoelaces crossed the threshold of our cell door and into the dayroom, they were on his heels like a pair of socks. Each time it happened, I would offer words of encouragement to him.

To separate cadres from general population, we received different colored uniforms. The cadres also got more recreation time and more freedom to move on the compound. This meant I could attend chapel services whenever I wanted instead of once every two weeks.

Christian services held at the chapel were inspiring. They ran three times a week and were led by outside pastors. There was no set schedule as far as who was coming, which made it even more exciting. Some pastors would bring their praise and worship teams. For me, this heightened the worship experience.

Brother Joe introduced me to the music director who subsequently asked me to fill the role of bass player. For me, playing my instrument is the best form of worshipping God. Who would have known when I picked up the bass guitar at age twelve that I would be ministering to men in prison through music? God knew and prepared me for it.

Let me encourage *you* to use your gifts for the Lord. If you have children, encourage them to do the same. God will use them in ways you cannot imagine, thus advancing His kingdom. Proverbs 18:16 says, *A man's gift makes room for him, And brings him before great men.* I can attest to this.

At the end of service, the pastor gave an invitation to accept Christ. After leading us in prayer, he said, "If this is the first time you have ever asked to be forgiven for your sins, please come forward." When six men rose to their feet and walked to the front, I could do nothing but cry.

I looked at these men, some young, some up in years, and I sat in deep thought. I was having a hard time digesting how they had never asked God to forgive them. By now, I have done it well over a million times. The difference between these men and my once feeble prayers was that their actions seemed to have come from the heart. It was evident by how they were crying and hugging one another.

2 Corinthians 7:10 (NIV) says, *Godly sorrow brings repentance that leads to salvation and leaves no regret, but worldly sorrow brings death.* No doubt this was why God allowed their entry to prison, to find Him.

Colossians 2:13,14 (ERV) says, *You were spiritually dead because of your sins and because you were not free from the power of your sinful self. But God gave you a new life together with Christ. He forgave all your sins. Because we broke God's laws, we owed a debt - a debt that listed all the rules we failed to follow. But God forgave us of that debt. He took it away and nailed it to the cross.*

I don't know if the men who accepted Christ that day fully understood the gift they had received, but one thing was certain, they were forgiven.

CHAPTER TWENTY-FIVE

WHERE THERE ARE PEOPLE, THERE IS PURPOSE

The harvest truly is plentiful, but the laborers are few. Therefore, pray the Lord of the harvest to send out laborers into His field. Matthew 9:37,38

The six men who received Christ that day at the chapel had a profound effect on me. It was impossible to look at the twelve hundred men at LORCI in the same way I had once looked at them. There was a harvest full of people to help. Time was of the essence.

In Romans 10:14,15, the apostle Paul wrote, *How then shall they call on Him in whom they have not believed? And how shall they believe in Him of whom they have not heard? And how shall they hear without a preacher? And how shall they preach unless they are sent?*

I felt the Holy Spirit leading me out of my comfort zone, telling me to roll up my sleeves and get to work. Initially, I was reluctant. I did not want to draw attention to myself; but, if I stayed hidden behind the cross of Jesus, that would not be a problem.

Going out and speaking life into offenders was an incredible feeling. Love, joy, excitement, inspiration, and truth all mixed to form a stew I would be serving for the Lord to the men.

With my ears tuned into the frequency of the Spirit and keeping a sober mind, He presented opportunities to witness daily. Sometimes a simple "God bless you" in passing would strike up a conversation. All it takes is a spark to light a fire.

It is so important that we remain busy for the Lord. Jesus did not redeem us with His blood so we could go into hibernation. He redeemed us so we could share His love with others.

An active Christian isa dangerous Christian to Satan. Let me say that again. *An active Christian is a dangerous Christian to Satan.* Satan knows any lazy or idle Christian will be easy pickings.

1 Peter 5:8 warns us to *Be sober, be vigilant; because your adversary the devil walks about like a roaring lion seeking whom he may devour.*

So... it's okay for Satan to be active and not us Christians? I don't think so. Once we accept Christ, we enlist in His army. What good is a soldier who goes into war and then refuses to fight? In the same way, I believe a lethargic Christian puts his life and the lives of those around him at risk.

Just like County Jail, men at LORCI gravitated toward me. With the Lord's help, I did my best to make the most of every opportunity without being pushy or preachy. I just wanted them to see there was a better way than the path some of them were taking.

One evening I was walking briskly back to the block when I

came upon four young men. I usually walk at a quick pace but slowed to their cadence. From what I heard, they were in the midst of debating, and it was not too difficult to figure out the topic: who had the better city. It was the same thing men at the county jail argued about all the time.

Eventually, one of them looked at me. "Where are you from?" I chuckled. Talk about déjà vu. It was County Jail all over again.

I waited until they quieted before answering. "It's not about where I'm from, it's about where I'm going," and then pointed to the sky. With no rebuttal, I knew their minds were churning. One of the men spoke and admitted that he needed to get back into church, prompting a head nod from the others. With the entrance of the cadre block just ahead, I invited them to a service at the chapel and said I would be praying for them.

I sensed the Lord calling me to do more, but I did not know what "more" entailed. In the most generic way possible, I knew to be ready to help whomever and whenever at a moment's notice (2 Timothy 4:2.) I prayed and asked the Holy Spirit to show me the way, and He did.

I was speaking to an offender and, prior to parting ways, asked if there was anything I could help him pray about. He unloaded more than I could remember so I grabbed a piece of paper to jot it down. That's when the Holy Spirit gave me an idea.

Because most prison pants have no pockets, I started carrying paper and pen in my shirt pocket. As the Holy Spirit moved in me, I would ask the person I was speaking with to write down their prayer requests. This happened increasingly, and I was shocked at how many people were willing to do it.

The job I had required me to walk building to building, so I was constantly moving on the yard. Many who had written prayer requests stopped me and testified how God was answering our prayers. This increased their faith and gave them a greater understanding of the power in prayer.

I was surprised the first time someone asked me to pray for them on the yard, in front of everybody. That was something I was not used to doing, and it began happening more and more: in the yard, the gym, library, chapel, and in the block. I treated it like a game of *Hot Potato*, only this was no game. They would come to me for help, and I would pass them to Jesus as fast as I could. My goal was to stay out the way.

To this day, I carry those prayer requests in my Bible. These men, some forgotten by society, were not forgotten by God. He was making Himself real to them through His love.

In what ways do you feel you can serve in the field of our Lord: volunteering at a local homeless shelter, getting involved in your church, praying more? Something you may want to consider is donating Christian books to your local jail or prison. Nearly all books provided come through donations.

Seek the Lord and He will direct you in ways to serve in His field. The harvest is ripe, but the workers are few. God is hiring. Will you work for Him? It's time we roll up our sleeves, get down in the dirt, and do our part to bring in our Lord's harvest.

CHAPTER TWENTY-SIX

SUBMISSION

Teach me to do your will, for you are my God; may your good Spirit lead me on level ground. Psalm 143:10 (NIV)

There was a lot of talk about Grafton Correctional Institution (GCI) when I was in County Jail. It was an honor camp, had great programs in which to get involved, and had a reputation for being one of the safest and most laid-back men's prisons in the United States. This made it difficult to get into, and it normally took quite a while for a transfer.

I asked around and learned the name and location of a person who had authority to transfer me. This was good news. The bad news was her office was off limits to offenders.

Painted on the ground of most prisons are red lines that have lettering with the slogan *OUT OF PLACE!* This is to let offenders know where they cannot go. Cross that line and a CO could write you an Out of Place ticket. Each ticket you receive for disrespect, fighting, contraband, disobeying a direct order and so forth, goes on your institutional record. It can have a negative effect on the possibility of early release or parole. Sometimes your prison record will get you into a prison of your choice rather than one they will blindly send you to. My record was spotless, and I hoped this would increase my chances of getting to GCI.

I spoke with my case manager about a transfer to GCI and learned I was ineligible because I did not have a High School Diploma or a General Education Diploma (GED). I figured not finishing high school would bite me in the rear, but the last place I expected it to happen was in prison. My case manager already given me the score, and it looked like *Team Policy* took the victory. However, I could not shake the unsettling feeling that remained. I had to act on it, and it would take a huge risk to do that.

With each step sending a nervous impulse through my body, I mentally crossed the line, then physically crossed it. I was now *OUT OF PLACE*. I approached her office and pulled against a locked door. I needed to be buzzed in. I pressed the buzzer. Nothing. The rapid beating of my heart made its way to my eardrums. "This is crazy!" I mumbled.

The secretary came to the door, "How can I help you?"

The words in my brain fought hard to send the words to my mouth, but the large lump in my throat prevented me from saying something eloquent. Instead, I croaked out a weak "I'm here to see Mrs. Stuart."

"Did she call for you?"

"Umm, no, she didn't but I only need a minute of her time," I urged, shaking in my state-issued Velcro shoes.

"I'll see if she wants to see you. Have a seat."

I hate sitting when my nerves are on edge. I would much rather pace and expend the nervous energy, but I complied.
Mrs. Stuart came to the door and stood looking all business. I rose to keep her from looking down on me.

"Mr. Parker, I should write you up. You know you're not supposed to be over here."

"I know, but I'm desperate and need your help."

I don't know where the boldness came from, but I politely slipped by her and made my way into her office. I expected a harsh rebuke and maybe a bunch of CO's rushing over. Instead, she followed md in and took a seat at her desk.

I voiced the reasons I wanted transferred then addressed the elephant in the room, my lack of education. Would you like to know what she said? Wait for it... wait... and while I waited for her to speak, she turned her back and made a phone call. After the call, she typed on her computer. "I just sent an email to Grafton. We should know within a couple of days whether or not they will accept you."

Whew! This little adventure of mine could have turned out bad. God had given me favor.

One week passed with no news. No biggie. A second week passed with no news. Now it was a big deal. Every thought that was the antithesis of faith entered my mind. Unfortunately, I gave heed to them all. *Maybe she emailed the wrong person. Maybe she hasn't checked her emails in a while.* These useless thoughts dominated my mind.

I returned to her office a few days later and she was even confused by the lack of response. "I don't know, Mr. Parker, we may need to come up with a Plan B."

I did not want to hear nothin' about "Plan B." Plan G... CI was the only plan I had in mind. I think I left her office more confused than she was. That confusion turned to frustration, which I directed toward God. I don't know why I continued to point a finger at Him.

The exact words I spewed out on the yard as I pouted like a spoiled child were, "God, I don't care if it *is not* Your will. I want to go to Grafton!" (I find myself chuckling while writing this. Granny always told me that God takes care of babies and fools, so I guess I was covered.)

God did not respond to my temper tantrum, which was probably for my own good. I came to my senses (again) and quickly asked Him (again) to forgive me for speaking to Him that way. This was another sign my relationship with God was growing. He was not just an imaginary genie in the sky. He was my friend. I felt comfortable communicating with Him, even if it was reckless at times.

One of my biggest struggles is patience. I have carried this flaw from childhood to adulthood. This was going to be a teachable moment.

Twenty-one days after my first meeting with Mrs. Stuart, I was physically tired from the footwork and mentally drained from the worry. That morning I threw my hands up in a sign of surrender and prayed, "God, You know how much I want transferred to Grafton. I have done everything I can do, and it's brought me nothing but grief. I know You have nothing but good plans for me, so I give this situation to You."

After the prayer, I climbed out of bed and got dressed. I hit the yard to do my job when a sudden urge to visit Mrs. Stuart struck me. I was apprehensive because I knew I was tap-dancing on her nerves, so I told myself this would be the last time I would show up at her door unannounced.

I entered with both arms raised and a smile on my face, "I come in peace."

The perplexed look on her face said, how did you know to come here, but her mouth said, "You're not going to believe this. Grafton has accepted you. I'm holding your transfer papers." What I saw was the biggest smile ever. "I'm not allowed to tell you when you'll be leaving (for security purposes), but you might want to start packing."

I wanted to hug her. However, physical contact is prohibited between staff and offenders, so I did my best to express my gratitude with words.

I walked to the block extra slow, taking in what had just occurred. Tears of joy sprang to my eyes as praises went up to God. He had given me a lesson on patience and submission simultaneously. Had I not let go of my will, I believe those three weeks of waiting would have taken much longer. He was in control, and the only thing I could do was submit.

Before entering, I looked up at the sky and thought of how God worked. It made me smile. "Well, played God. Well played."

CHAPTER TWENTY-SEVEN

BLESSED AND HIGHLY FAVORED

But while Joseph was there in prison, the Lord was with him; he showed him kindness and granted him favor in the eyes of the prison warden. Genesis 39:21 (NIV)

The first thing I noticed at GCI was the median age. It was higher than where I had previously been. To me, that was a good sign, because when men typically age through the system, they become less violent and less apt to commit other crimes against other offenders, like stealing. I got the vibe it was a laid-back spot.

Unfortunately, living arrangements in my building were a total shock. Gone were the days of living in a cell. I would be living in a dorm with about two hundred other men. There was no privacy, absolutely none! The showers and toilets were also devoid of privacy, with lines oftentimes for both.
When I heard the other eight buildings of GCI consisted of cells,

and one of them was a faith-based honor dorm, I immediately put in a request to move and prayed fervently about it.

In the meantime, I found my way to the school to inquire about obtaining my GED.

The secretary's door was propped open, so I went in (there was no red line for me to ignore BUT I didn't see the note taped to a wall that read *No Office Hours*). When I introduced myself to the secretary, a short, husky man stepped out of his office and ingratiated his way into our conversation.

"I know who you are," he said with an investigative demeanor. "What I don't know is how you got over here." His voice was calm but the scowl on his face said more than the words coming from his mouth. It appeared he took offense to my being there at GCI. I felt the next thing he would try to do was challenge me to a duel, but before I could ready myself, he shot first.

"The type of transfer listed on your file is some sort of clerical error."

"Interesting," I replied, unsure of what to say.

He walked away without notice and, by the sound of it, was in his office pecking away on a keyboard like a mad scientist. The secretary scrunched her lips, shrugged her shoulders, and shook her head as if to say, *what's his problem?*

He called my name, "Since you're here, I might as well get you enrolled in class." Then his curiosity got the best of him. Looking up from the keyboard, he tossed his custom Ray Ban glasses on a pile of papers, and said, "So how did you get over here?"

I could see the suspense was killing him, so I saved the useless banter and cut right into the center of the steak. "By bus," I teased with a smile.

The case manager, who was much nicer, asked the same question. I simply said, "The favor of God." She paused, gave a curious smile, and replied, "Amen!" Before I left her office, she gave me the most encouraging words I had heard in a long time. "You're going to do great things when you get out of here. I can tell!" She had no idea how much I prayed her prophecy would come to fruition.

Next on my agenda was to get involved at the chapel. I linked up with the praise team and looked forward to playing in the band, but there was only one problem, I no longer had an instrument. My plan was to purchase one and have it sent to me. God had a better plan.

Word had spread on the compound that I played bass guitar. One day someone came to me and handed me one. Again, I was apprehensive. I tried to back out of it by telling the man that I am left-handed, and he replied, "I know, that's why I converted it for you." ...only God.

Six weeks later, I moved to the faith-based block. It became evident this was where God wanted me, where I would no longer be in the role of a leader like I was at LORCI. I would now be a student.

Some of the men had been locked up before I was even born, and the more I spoke with them, the more I realized getting to Grafton was not as easy for them as it was for me. One man said it took him ten years to transfer, another nine years, and finally four and half years for the third man. It had only taken me twenty-five days. The favor of God.

I was there for a reason.

CHAPTER TWENTY-EIGHT

MATTERS OF THE HEART

Delight yourself also in the Lord, And He shall give you the desires of your heart. Psalm 37:4

I spent a lot of time writing and realized God instilled in me a gift to write. What a shame I did not recognize it before I was locked up. I first noticed it in the county jail; Mom noticed it when I was younger. She would often ask me to write poems for her. All I needed was a topic and I could usually put something together in a timely manner. I guess the latent talent just needed jarred loose and prison was the jarring agent of change.

The Holy Spirit directed me to write a blessing journal. This would allow me to keep track of the many ways God blessed me. I would read it when things got rough, and it would boost my faith. It was a reminder that if God did it before, He would do it again. He does not change (see Malachi 3:6). Sometimes we must encourage *ourselves*. If *we* don't do it, why should we expect anyone else to do it?

It is so easy to become disgruntled about life, especially in prison, but if we stop complaining and start saying thank you, it might just change our attitude. I challenge *you* to write a blessing list. If you do, I don't believe you'll see your problems the same.

The Holy Spirit also directed me to create a prayer journal. In it, I wrote the needs of others in addition to my own. Seeing this on paper made it seem more real.

Here are two entries from my prayer journal I would like to share:

March 1, 2019:
"God, make me into a great Christian writer for *Your* glory."
March 26, 2019:
"God, make a way for novel (Will You Be Ready) to be published. Work a miracle, Jesus."

The writing bug got hold of me and never let go. Now my attention focused on getting published. I started watching TV and reading magazine articles about publishing and was gut punched when I saw the prices. This discouragement was all encompassing. There was no way I could afford it, especially while in prison. If it were to happen, it would take a miracle.

Several months after the family day at LORCI, Jean and I began corresponding through letters. I was taken aback by her undeniable love for God and her love for me. I spent most of my life seeking approval from family, friends, and women I barely knew, but I never felt the need to put on airs with Jean. She accepted me for who I was.

When we met, I had no idea she was in the process of writing a series of biblically based children's books. This piqued my interest because of our shared interest, writing.

We were using the prison's email service to communicate, and the message I received from her on February 6, 2020, was the start of God's plan for my life. It said, in part, "The gentleman I can arrange for you to meet is Tony Agnesi. He's a book author, radio host, and is a Christian who specializes in prison ministry. That checks a lot of boxes. He'll understand your talents and your situation in life as a Christian."

She passed along his contact information, and Tony and I began corresponding. Right away he sent me copies of his three books. In them, Tony shares experiences he's had while helping the underprivileged and incarcerated.

I had just finished reading one of his books and was so inspired that, in my next letter to him, I attached several chapters of this book, *Broken & Restored*, which I had just started to write a few weeks prior. On, December 18, 2020, this was his response:

"I spent a great deal of time going over the first four chapters of your book. Michael, you have a gift for storytelling. I was held by your words. If you promise to keep writing and follow through on completing the book, I will cover the cost. I want nothing in return but to see God use your book to launch your ministry."

I am glad I was on my bunk, or I may have passed out. This was one of the few times in prison that I cried openly like a baby. They were happy tears. It's hard to find the words to thank God for His goodness, mercy, grace, and faithfulness. The best way we can show our love for Him is to follow in His steps.

A few weeks later, God put the icing on the cake when I learned the reason Tony was so open to helping me. It was because he owned a publishing company. God's right hand of favor was raised high for me, and I am so grateful.

This took me back to an encounter I had in County Jail. I was in the cell, standing on the bed, trying to get a glimpse of the outside world. I had to shield my eyes because of the sun's glare. That was when the Holy Spirit spoke to my mind and said, "Your future is bright because it's guided by the Son (Jesus)!"

After this encounter with Tony, I knew God's plan was in motion.

CHAPTER TWENTY-NINE

ANXIETY

Do not be anxious about anything, but in every situation, by prayer and petition, with thanksgiving, present your requests to God. Philippians 4:6 (NIV)

From the beginning, prison took the anxiety I had and raised it to a completely new level. I worried about everything. Fear of the unknown and what could happen to me on the inside, the wellbeing of my loved ones on the outside, all keeping my mind racing. I reverted to my old ways of burying my feelings and worried myself to sleep at night.

The first thing I did was talk to the medical staff about switching my medication since I believed it was no longer doing its job. They agreed and made the change. Looking back, the mistake I made was obvious. There was nothing wrong with talking to a doctor, but prayer should have been my first response rather than my last resort. I continued to beat my head against the wall until deciding to consult God.

While studying the Bible, I came across Philippians 4:6. This was the prescription I needed first. I responded with a simple prayer: "God, Your Word tells me not to worry about anything and at times I am worrying about everything. Unless You help me, I'm going to be on these pills for the rest of my life. I don't want that. Please help me."

It was not until a few days later that the Holy Spirit revealed that my inconsistent prayer and Bible reading triggered my anxiety. I went through my journal and noticed on days I read the Bible I was not anxious. On days I worried, I did not read at all. This was a no brainer.

Over time, positive changes were more frequent and more noticeable. On nights the enemy tried to rock me to sleep with worry, I would recite Scripture until I fell asleep. Scripture became the sheep I counted.

Doing all I knew to do, and following the Holy Spirit's direction, I spoke with a doctor and requested to be taken off my medication. After some persuading, they agreed.

From that moment forward, I have not taken a single pill for anxiety or depression. God completely set me free. I mean, who goes to prison and gets delivered from anxiety in an environment where it is the norm? Thank You, Jesus!

As part of our agreement, I continued meeting with a counselor to ensure I stayed on track. Talking about my feelings wasn't something I was comfortable with, but the more I did the better I felt.

I shared with the counselor that my faith in Jesus was the reason I was doing so well. That was when he confessed to being a believer as well. It's good to know there are believers working in the prison system.

We spent much of our sessions talking about the Lord. Once he said, "Sometimes I wonder who the doctor is and who is the patient." I give credit to the transforming power only found in our risen Savior.

CHAPTER THIRTY

PROMPTINGS FROM THE HOLY SPIRIT

However, when He, the Spirit of truth, has come, He will guide you into all truth; for He will not speak on His own authority, but whatever He hears He will speak; and He will tell you things to come. John 16:13

Several weeks before I transferred to GCI, I met Kenny. Kenny was a stocky, African American man in his thirty's. The respect he showed others was one of the things that made an impression on me.

In prison you meet guys and don't question why they are there, but there are a select few who make you scratch your head and wonder how they got there. Kenny was one of those guys.

When I learned about my transfer, I kept it quiet but shared it with Kenny. I knew he had more time to serve than I did and wanted him to know I would always be his brother in Christ. We swapped information and I promised to write.

Three months after I arrived at GCI, I had every intention of writing him, but time seemed to slip away. Writing has always come easy, but when I sat to gather my thoughts to write Kenny, I had a hard time putting the words together. This happened twice and both letters ended up in the trash.

Seven months had passed when Kenny came to mind in a forceful way. Neither of us had written to each other. It was not a fleeting thought, but a heavy burden on my mind and heart. I knew the Holy Spirit was prompting me to write.

I still remember where I was when I made the decision to sit and write Kenny. I was determined not to get up until the letter was complete. Leaning on the Holy Spirit for His words, not mine, I wrote Kenny. This was his response.

Brother Parker:
You don't know how badly I needed this letter today. I tell you; God does everything in His perfect timing.
You said that you started a letter for me back in January, but God knew I would need it today.
I woke up this morning with my faith feeling ripped from my soul and the conversation I had with God wasn't pleasant. I had a feeling of hopelessness, but God showed me through your letter that He is still with me and has my back like He promised...
There was never a doubt I would remember you. I know God placed you on my path for a reason and maybe today was that reason. Through this time, I have been battling some things. Giving up has been an option, even up to this very day. My prayers seem to fall flat but your words have encouraged me. I read your letter to my girl, and she broke out in tears. It gave her a newfound hope as well. Thank you for being obedient to His Word. You are a true brother. Please keep in touch. Kenny.

This letter rocked me to my core and put me on my knees in prayer. I sobbed, thanking God for allowing me to touch the hearts of Kenny and his girlfriend.

There is no place the love of God won't travel to touch a soul. I have often wondered what may have happened had I not yielded to the Holy Spirit's prompting.

Have you ever sensed the Holy Spirit's promptings? How did you respond? Do you know that delayed obedience *is* disobedience? When the Holy Spirit prompts us, we are to obey at once. The way we respond may not only impact our lives but the lives of others.

CHAPTER THIRTY-ONE

BE THE LIGHT

Let your light shine before others, that they may see your good deeds and glorify your Father in heaven.
Matthew 5:16 (NIV)

In prison, there is a glut of self-proclaimed Master Chef's. There are several in every block. I must admit, some of the food guys prepare is pretty good considering they only have a microwave at their disposal. One guy earned this title. We decided to cook a meal, so I skipped lunch to help put it together. It took way longer than expected and by the time it was done, my stomach was touching my back. I was starving!

I returned to the cell with food in hand, closed the door with every intention of digging in until unexpectedly my appetite vanished. I stood wondering what to do so I put the food on the bed, grabbed a book, and headed to a table in the dayroom.

In less than two minutes, a twenty-five-year-old man sat down and said, "Read me something." He was used to seeing me in the dayroom with my Bible, but this time I grabbed a book about what else, writing.

"This isn't a Bible, but I can quote you a scripture." Before I could say anything else, he interrupted.

"Did you know Jesus was born in a manger because there was no room for Him in the inn?" I did my best not to look surprised.

He continued.

"I have three brothers with Bible names. My brother Luke has been going through some stuff and that's why I decided to read Luke."

Another name he mentioned was Jeremiah, so I shared how God spoke to me through Jeremiah 29:11 while in County Jail. I felt the presence of the Holy Spirit and sensed the young man was clinging to my every word. The dayroom was noisy and full of people yet if seemed as though we were the only ones there.

"I'm trying to do better," he declared. "I've asked God to forgive me for things I've done, and I think He's forgiven me halfway. Once I get out and accomplish some positive things, then I think He'll forgive me the rest of the way."

This was a God moment. I realized why my appetite had vanished. God was going to use me to plant seeds of truth in this young man's heart. What an honor.

"Brother," I explained, "God doesn't do *anything* halfway. If you were sincere when you asked Him to forgive you, then you *ARE* forgiven. Just believe."

He was quiet. He looked over his shoulders, leaned in, and then whispered, "But what if I shot somebody?"

His sincerity nearly broke me. I clinched my jaw to keep my composure.

"He will forgive you," I whispered back, fighting the tears.

I shared how Moses killed a man and God still used him a fantastic way. His face lit up, "Really?"

"Yeah, man. Moses was a gangster," I joked.

I also let him know that there is nothing we can do to earn our salvation. Jesus did it all for us.

The conversation ended with him saying, "I'm gonna ask God to forgive me one more time and this time I'm gonna believe it."

We don't always know who is watching us. As followers of Christ, we have the privilege of representing Him. How we live reflects how some people see Jesus. If we allow the Holy Spirit to shine brightly through us, it will draw the lost to the cross.

Have you ever been around someone and the smell of their perfume or cologne grabbed your attention? You might even ask what they are wearing. In the same way, followers of Christ should be attractive to others. When people come around us, they should be intrigued by our lives and wonder what fragrance we're wearing. What makes us different? When they ask, that's our opportunity to tell them about Jesus.

The light a *true* Christian has is often imitated but never duplicated. In it is the power of God, which becomes a beacon of hope for those who are lost and searching for The Light. With the world around us growing darker by the day, it might be easy to lose hope, but don't give up. Always remember: the darker the night, the brighter the light. *BE THE LIGHT!*

CHAPTER THIRTY-TWO

IDENTITY CRISIS

If you are the Son of God command that these stones become bread. Matthew 4:3

The opening scripture depicts the moment after Jesus fasted forty days and forty nights. He was physically weak and naturally hungry, and what better time for Satan to tempt Him.

Out of all the ways Jesus was tempted, Matthew only penned the three found in verses three, six, and nine. In each instance, Satan attacked Christ's identity. It should not have come as a surprise when he went after mine.

One of the many things in prison I had to get used to was being identified by Parker. Everywhere but prison, I was "Mike" or

"Michael".

The sameness with which days run together in prison is mind numbing. To single one day out over another means something extraordinary must have happened. The first time I noticed an offender arguing with a CO was one of those times. The CO screamed "What did you say, *INMATE*?" Used in this context, it is degrading to the offender. The only way I can explain how I felt was the same way I would if I had heard somebody use a racial slur.

The next day I was walking to the chapel. A storm was brewing, and the wind was howling in every direction. I thought of Jesus calming the wind and the raging sea with three simple words and decided to try it (see Mark 4:37-39). At the top of my lungs, I shouted at the wicked wind, "PEACE, BE STILL," and guess what happened. Nothing. That's right, nothing. If anything, the wind howled back in laughter. With the wind came a discouragement that blew in allowing the enemy to speak to my mind. "See, you're nothing like your Father," but before I could process the thought, the Spirit of God spoke through my mouth and said, "You can *be* the peace in the storm." It happened so quick I gasped.

In the midst of this spiritual storm (prison), I did not have to let the storm inside me. If I kept my eyes on Jesus, He would give me peace and allow me to be an example of peace to those around me.

It was not until later that I noticed Satan had identified God as my Father. I had to smile. I caught on to his tactic of mixing truth with false, something he mastered in the Garden of Eden (see Genesis 3:1-7). That did not deter him, though. Over the next few days, the persistence of his attacks grew.

Whenever a package is mailed from prison, it needs a cash slip attached to it with the offender's information. All cash slips require the signature of a staff member to mail it, and now that you know this... I was mailing a package to my daughters and stood at the CO desk to receive the signature. She signed it. I walked away. Ten minutes later I returned with a different package and stood by after she took the cash slip.

"Did you notice I signed my name different this time than I did before?" she bragged, admiring her penmanship.

"No, I wasn't paying attention."

"I did it so you guys can't copy my signature."

I did not know where this was going, so I buckled up for the ride.

"I'm one of the good guys," I joked.

"Yeah... that's what you all say. You're an inmate. I get to leave here."

I pointed to my head. "I get to leave here too," meaning my mind was not trapped inside the prison walls.

She tried to clarify. "No! I get to go home every night and get into my bed. You stay here."

I felt she mocked me using a baby voice. I was becoming frustrated, so I extended my hand, took my cash slip, and walked away. Her words bothered me because I was already questioning myself.

The last straw came when I was on the yard and saw one of the institutional big wigs escorting female guests to another part of the prison. I walked toward them on the same sidewalk. As I neared, I instinctively thought, *you're an inmate. You don't want to scare these women*, and I veered onto the grass, hoping to make them feel comfortable.

Whatever I felt I had to do was no longer important. I turned around and went to my cell to talk with God. I opened my Bible to see who God says I am in Him. 2 Corinthians 5:2, I am an ambassador for Christ, John 15:15, I am His friend. 2 Corinthians 5:21, I am the righteousness of God.

This *is* who I am in Christ. When the Holy Spirit reminded me of this it was game over. Satan did not stop fighting me, but he did have to change his plan of attack.

When we know who we are and whose we are, we become spiritual savages against Satan and his pathetic kingdom. Whatever you have done in your past does not define who you are. In fact, it can be a catalyst for your future.

If you have been made new in Christ, you are in His image. Stand tall and walk with confidence because you represent the Most High God.

CHAPTER THIRTY-THREE

DIVINE INTERVENTION

And the Lord (Jesus) said, 'Simon, Simon! Indeed, Satan has asked for you, that he may sift you as wheat. But I have prayed for you, that your faith should fail not; and when you have returned to Me, strengthen your brethren. Luke 22:31,32

Each time I read this I get emotional. Jesus is telling Peter that Satan is coming for him, but He intervened on his behalf. I imagine Jesus praying something like this:
Father, I know Peter is going to deny Me three times, cut off Malchus' ear, abandon Me in the garden when I needed him the most, and deny me three times, but Father don't let him lose faith in Me. Restore him and give him power to strengthen his brothers.

Peter was explosive, impulsive, and short-tempered. Jesus saw Peter's potential and knew he would be a powerhouse for His Father's kingdom. I can relate to this divine intervention.

As you can imagine there are a lot of rules in prison. Some I feel are ridiculous, some need revised, while others are completely necessary.

One rule in Ohio prisons is if an offender and staff member knew each other prior to prison, the staff member must disclose it. If they decided not to and the offender does not say anything, all is well. If the relationship is disclosed, however, the consequences would be the offender would be moved to another prison. This rule, called *establishing*, was put in place to eliminate the chance of the offender being shown favoritism, among other things. I have seen this happen to several offenders, so it is a rule taken seriously.

It was February, and the prison calendar was filled with events to celebrate Black History Month. Our Deputy Warden had arranged for a pastor to hold service in the chapel. The praise team I was a member of would be opening the event.

During our sound check, the pastor walked in with our Sergeant, Deputy Warden, and a few other employees. When I saw the pastor, it felt like I knew him.

To start the service, the Deputy Warden came to the microphone and announced the guest pastor. When she said his name, I realized he pastored the church I had played at for two and a half weeks then quit. The Deputy Warden also shared that she and the Sergeant were members of his church.

I sat in my seat and gave an audible, "WOW!" I never knew why I had the urge to quit when I did but God made it clear in that moment.

The size of his church was small and had I followed through playing there, I am certain I would have befriended these two women and been in violation of the establishing rule. God intervened.

Even though I was not following Christ during the time I played at the pastor's church, God knew I would end up in prison, particularly GCI. This confirmed that I was exactly where God wanted me to be. At GCI.

CHAPTER THIRTY-FOUR

JESUS IS THE ANSWER

Jesus said to him, 'I am the way, the truth, and the life. No one comes to the Father except through Me. John 14:6

God was doing wonderful works in my life and left no stone unturned in doing so. Every issue I had, big or small, He had addressed in some form or fashion. I would have never thought in a million years that prison would be the place God would bring the pain of losing Dad to light to help me through it.

The stress of prison did a number on me. I could tell by the gray hairs sprouting in the middle of my head. I had to chuckle. Father Time had finally caught me and had me in a bear hug. I wondered if Dad had gray hair at age thirty-six, then I remembered he did not live past age thirty.

I shook my head in sadness and found myself getting worked up, and not in a good way. Thinking about the man who took

Dad's life put me in a mental funk over the next few days. It was not until I opened the Bible that the Holy Spirit gave me a hard slap in the face of reality, and He used two short verses to do it.

Ephesians 4:31,32 (NIV), *Get rid of all bitterness, rage, anger, brawling and slander, along with every form of malice. Be kind and compassionate to one another, forgiving each other, just as in Christ God forgave you.*

I got quiet before the Lord as His conviction covered me. He replayed the situation that led to my incarceration. I was no different from my dad's killer. Had it been a few seconds longer, I would be in the same shoes, but for the grace of God.

If that was not enough, the Holy Spirit revealed that the same hurt I felt about missing Dad was the same hurt my daughters felt from missing me. Talk about giving it to me straight. Once I took the log of hypocrisy out of my eye, I could see things more clearly (see Matthew 7:5).

Now that God had cut me open, it was time for Him to bandage me up. The chaplain announced he was starting a five-week class on grief. I signed up. In the class, I learned ways to cope and gained biblical knowledge to help the healing process. My main source of healing came from the Bible. God's Word is all-powerful and sharper than any double-edged sword. Not only does it cut like a knife, but it also heals. Slowly but surely, God was breaking the chains of the enemy off my life.

I was speaking to the chaplain at the end of a church service. I knew he was a poem enthusiast and I told him that I had written a poem about my dad. When he asked if I wanted to share it in a service, I respectfully declined.

Several months had passed and he asked again. This time, I felt a nudge from the Holy Spirit and agreed. As I walked to the podium, I started having second thoughts. *Did I hear the Spirit correctly*, was one I wrestled. Before reading the poem, I gave a brief overview of Dads life and his death. Then I whispered a silent prayer, released a deep sigh, and began.

THE ANSWER:

As a child, I had more questions than answers and when I asked no one knew what to say.
Questions like, why was my dad killed three days before my ninth birthday?
I lost my hero. He was gone. As a child this seemed too much to bear.
I was angry, confused. God, where were You as he lay there dying? Did You even care?
Of course He cared. He too suffered a great loss.
He sent His only Son Jesus to save us from our sins, and watched Him die on an Old Rugged Cross.
Yes, He could have stopped His Son from dying and spared my dad as well.
But He allowed it and I am so glad He did because Dad is in glory and not in hell.
Dad, one day I will see you again. Like you, I too have found The Answer.
His name is Jesus Christ, King of kings and Lord of lords and I will follow Him no matter.
No longer do I ponder on the 'what, why's, or how's' of this life because I know *Who* holds my future in His hands. Whether I am in a valley or on a mountaintop, I have peace knowing God has a plan.
Not every day will be easy which is why we must walk by faith and not by sight.
When we do this, *nothing* can defeat us, for we are *more* than conquerors, it is a fixed fight.

This is all contingent upon our relationship with Christ and we can go as deep we choose.
The secret is to get into God's Word and God's Word will get into you.
Lord, any issues I have I lay at your feet, for You are my Master.
I know that in Your presence, *all* my problems will shift into praise for You and You alone are *THE ANSWER*.

Getting through this was harder than expected. As the tears streamed down my face, a couple brothers came and put their hand on my shoulders in support as I continued to read. I apologized for being emotional and they responded with a standing ovation. That really touched me. I told them that it was not easy but with God's help, I was able to forgive the man who took Dad's life. I hope to tell him so face to face.

Before leaving the stage, I asked the men to bow their heads as I prayed for Dad's killer. I asked God to touch his heart so he could find forgiveness for his soul.

I heard sniffling, as I took my seat, and witnessed several men wiping tears from their eyes, some of them murderers.

A few months later, someone stopped me in the chow hall and said, "Every time I see you, I think about the story you shared about your dad. It was powerful and you need to keep telling it." I agreed.

Hear me when I say God cares about every detail in your life. Only He could have started the process of healing me from three decades of hurt. I still get sad at times, but I have the assurance of knowing I will see my daddy again.

Death you tried and failed, all because of Jesus.

CHAPTER THIRTY-FIVE

RESTORED

Writing this book has been an adventure and a challenge. I wrestled with what stories to include and which to leave out. This book, however, would not be complete if I did not include the dream God gave me. Some advised me not to include it, that it sounded too perfect, too good, to be true. To describe it, instead, as a deep thought.

I would have to say I would have none of that, for God has spoken to me three times in this way, in a dream. I chose this one, and you will understand.

I was in my cell trying to read the Bible but found myself skimming over the pages. My mind was busy worrying about how I would bounce back from such a low point as prison.

I lay on the lumpy mattress overcome with worry. Sinking into deep thought, I drifted off to sleep and had a dream, which was like no other I have ever had...

I was standing underneath a tree, enjoying shade from its

branches, while staring into an empty field. The atmosphere was incredibly peaceful. I did not know where I was, but I wanted to stay there forever. As I took in the scene, I saw another me walking into the frame from the left side of the field. I appeared to be walking aimlessly and without direction.

The *me* in the field saw someone else off in the distance and out of frame. I pushed from the tree and stepped far enough to see what the me in the field had seen. It was Jesus, and He was gazing back at the me in the field.
I sensed the indecisive emotions of the me in the field. Me did not know whether to bow, cry, worship, or do nothing. Suddenly, Jesus opened His arms.

The me in the field took off running toward Him at full speed. Before me got to Him, me tripped and fell at Jesus' feet, breaking into a million pieces.

I stepped further from the tree, toward the broken me and Jesus, wondering what would happen next.

Jesus did not move, rather, He stood there looking down at the shattered mess my life had become. I noticed His head turning back and forth, studying the pieces.

Slowly, Jesus stooped down, picked up a piece, then another, and began putting them together. This went on for quite some time. As I watched from a distance, I wondered why He did not just speak a word and put me together at once.

Hearing my silent thought, Jesus said, "I want to use My hands to put you back together. I love you that much. You are valuable to Me. My undying love for you will be the glue that keeps you together."

When He finished speaking, I woke from the dream. I must have been crying in my sleep because tears were already streaming down my cheeks. I knew without a doubt my life was literally in the hands of Almighty God. All I had to do, no, all I should have been doing the whole time was trust in Him and He would put my life back together and better than it was before.

And so, it has been. God has been restoring my life one piece at a time after these five long years.

Deuteronomy 8:2,3 (NIV) best describes these years.

Remember how the Lord your God led you all the way in the wilderness these forty years, to humble and test you in order to know what was in your heart, whether or not you would keep his commands. He humbled you... to teach you that man does not live on bread alone but on every word that comes from the mouth of the Lord.

God used prison to humble me, not to harm me.

Psalm 119:71 (NIV) *It was good for me to be afflicted so that I might learn your decrees (commands).*

Prison changed my life for the better. It is where I developed an insatiable appetite, appreciation, and love for the Holy Spirit. I would *never* have left prison an overcomer without Him. It would have been impossible.

Prison is where God would heal me of so many past wounds, one piece at a time. Though some scars remain, such as my criminal record, may they only add to my testimony.

Prison is where I developed a trusting relationship with God. It is where I learned to close my eyes and fall backwards into His arms.

As I finalize this book, the Holy Spirit reminds me once again of Paul's journey to Damascus. It was not until he lost his sight that he was able to see... so I pen these words in my Bible:

"God had to lock me up to set me free."

I entered prison broken, but I left RESTORED!

~ Amen

REFERENCE LIST

Chapter 1: Romans 3:23 NKJV

Chapter 2: Philippians 4:7 KJV

Chapter 5: Psalm 101:7 NIV
Chapter 5: Malachi 3: 8-11 NKJV

Chapter 6: Proverbs 29:23 NKJV
Chapter 6: Mark 5:5 NKJV
Chapter 6: Proverbs 11:14 NKJV

Chapter 7: Matthew 11:28 NKJV

Chapter 8: John 11:25 NKJV
Chapter 8: 1 Samuel 16:7 NKJV
Chapter 8: Mark 16, 17, 18 NKJV
Chapter 8: Mark 5:25-34 NKJV

Chapter 12: Romans 5: 7, 8 ERV
Chapter 12: Ephesians 2: 8, 9 NKJV
Chapter 12: Hebrews 9:22 NIV
Chapter 12: Romans 6:23 ERV
Chapter 12: John 6:44 NKJV
Chapter 12: John 16:8 NKJV

Chapter 12: 1 John 1:9 NKJV
Chapter 12: 2 Corinthians 3:17 NIV

Chapter 14: Jude 1:4 NIV
Chapter 14: John 10:10 NKJV
Chapter 14: Proverbs 3:5, 6, NKJV
Chapter 15: 1 Peter 5:7 NIV
Chapter 15: James 15:16 NKJV
Chapter 16: Ephesians 4:26 NKJV
Chapter 16: Judges 14-17 NKJV

Chapter 17: 2 Corinthians 5:17 NKJV
Chapter 17: 1 Thessalonians 5:22 KJV
Chapter 17: 1 Corinthians 6:9 KJV
Chapter 17: Matthew 6:33 KJV
Chapter 17: Luke 1:37 NKJV
Chapter 17: Luke 18:16, 17 NIV
Chapter 17: Galatians 5:7 NIV
Chapter 17: Matthew 12:34b NKJV
Chapter 17:Genesis 4:7b NIV

Chapter 18: Acts 9:1-9 NKJV

Chapter 19: John 3:16 NKJV

Chapter 20: Song of Songs 2:15 NIV
Chapter 20: Psalm 40:13-15 NIV
Chapter 20: Psalm 18:30b NKJV
Chapter 20: Jeremiah 29:11 NIV

Chapter 21: Romans 8:28 NKJV

Chapter 22: Philippians 4:19 NKJV
Chapter 22: Psalm 46:10 NKJV

Chapter 23: Luke 12:7 NKJV
Chapter 23: James 4:8 NKJV
Chapter 23: Luke 12:6, 7 NIV
Chapter 23: Matthew 10:29 NKJV

Chapter 24: Luke 7:48 NKJV
Chapter 24: Proverbs 18:16 NKJV
Chapter 24: 2 Corinthians 7:10 NIV
Chapter 24: Colossians 2:13, 14 ERV
Chapter 25: Matthew 9:37, 38 NKJV
Chapter 25: Romans 10:14, 15 NKJV
Chapter 25: 1 Peter 5:8 NKJV

Chapter 26: Psalm 143:10 NIV

Chapter 27: Genesis 39:21 NIV

Chapter 28: Psalm 37:4 NIV

Chapter 29: Philippians 4:6 NIV

Chapter 30: John 16:13 NKJV

Chapter 31: Matthew 5:16 NIV
Chapter 31: Isaiah 64:6 NIV

Chapter 32: Matthew 4:3 NKJV
Chapter 32: Mark 4:37-39 NKJV
Chapter 32: Genesis 3:1-7 NKJV
Chapter 32: 2 Corinthians 5:20 NKJV
Chapter 32: John 15:15 NKJV
Chapter 32: 2 Corinthians 5:21 NKJV

Chapter 33: Luke 22:31, 32 NKJV

Chapter 34: John 14:6 NKJV
Chapter 34: Ephesians 4: 31, 32 NIV
Chapter 34: Matthew 7:5 NKJV

Chapter 35: Deuteronomy 8:2, 3 NIV
Chapter 35: Psalm 119:71 NIV

ACKNOWLEDGEMENTS

First, I would like to thank my Lord and Savior, Jesus Christ. Without Him, I would not have a testimony. It is through His death and resurrection that I have been redeemed and made new. Thank You for loving me.

Alex LeFevre: This all started with you. Thank you for sharing your mom with me at our family day event.

Jean LeFevre: Thank you for believing in me when I did not believe in myself. No one would be reading this if it weren't for you. Your encouraging words propelled me to pursue writing. God sent you when I needed you the most. I love you very much. God bless you and your husband, Greg. P.S. Thank you for feeding the sparrows on my behalf during my incarceration.

Tony Agnesi: Thank you for taking the time to read my story and believing in it. You are the ram in the bush that God supplied to make this book possible. Your words in our letters and the words in your books have helped me see the love of God in a new light. Thank you for "Walking the talk!"

Lynde Kosko: Thank you for the hard work and time you put into designing this book. Your attention to detail and dedication separates you from the crowd of graphic designers. God bless you and all that you touch.

Christiana Cacciato: *The Green Photograph*, thank you for photographing the headshots for this book and the extra photos you took of my daughters and me. You were a joy to work with.

Thomas Poindexter: Special thanks to you. You were my hands and feet during my incarceration. Without your willingness to transfer files, and endurance to withstand a persistent cousin, this would not have been possible. You are a godsend. I love you, Cuz.

   Michael Swiergosz: "Swiergosz," you taught me so much about writing. When I didn't feel like writing, you knocked on my cell door, pointed in the direction of the study room and said, "Let's go!" You are more than a friend; you are my brother for life! I love you. P.S. I couldn't have passed my GED exam without your tutoring!

   My siblings: Thank you for always taking my calls and for your financial support. You are the best siblings I have ever had.

   Mom: Without you, I don't know where I would be. You have been a constant source of comfort and support, even when I did not deserve it. I love you.

   Grandma: I find it hard to express just how much you mean to me. You are the air that flows into my lungs and the blood that flows through my veins. I look forward to spending eternity with you in heaven when that time comes.

   A special thanks to my family and friends who supported me through prayers and by other means during my most trying times. It truly takes a village. I pray God bursts a cloud of blessings over you and showers you with His best.

NOTES

NOTES